Introduction to Library Research in French Literature

*Introduction to Library Research
in French Literature*
Robert K. Baker

This book is an introduction to the complexities of library research for the student of French literature. Chapter 1 addresses the structure of the modern American academic library, giving particular attention to the exploitation of information in the card catalog, interlibrary loans, and the reference function. Chapter 2 is a selective bibliographic guide to the more important information resources (dictionaries, encyclopedias, bibliographies, etc.) likely to be found in the medium to large college or university library. Each title listed in this section is annotated as to scope and coverage, and the introduction to each type of reference tool includes a list of standard library subject headings for further library research. The final chapter provides practical suggestions on how to "get ready for research" on a term paper, as well as suggestions for further readings that explain the purposes and methodology of literary scholarship.

Robert Baker is reference librarian at Spokane Community College; he was previously assistant librarian at Gonzaga University. Mr. Baker, who holds B.A. and M.A. degrees in French, as well as an M.L.S. and Certificate of Specialization in College and University Librarianship, has taught both French and library research methodology courses at the University of California, Los Angeles.

Introduction to Library Research in French Literature

Robert K. Baker

Westview Press • Boulder, Colorado

A Westview Special Study

Copyright © 1978 by Westview Press, Inc.

Published in 1978 in the United States of America by

Westview Press, Inc.
5500 Central Avenue
Boulder, Colorado 80301
Frederick A. Praeger, Publisher and Editorial Director

Library of Congress Cataloging in Publication Data
Baker, Robert K   1946-
    Introduction to library research in French literature.
    (A Westview special study)
    Includes index.
    1. French literature--Bibliography.   2. Reference
books--French literature--Bibliography.   3. Bibliog-
raphy--Bibliography--French literature.   4. Libraries--
Handbooks, manuals, etc.   I. Title.
Z2171.B34 [PQ103]   016.84   77-18074
ISBN 0-89158-082-4 (paper)   ISBN 0-89158-060-3 (cloth)

Printed and bound in the United States of America

To my friends

CONTENTS

FIGURES

ACKNOWLEDGMENTS

A number of gracious colleagues and friends
have taken the time to read and comment on sections
of this work: Robert Vosper, UCLA Graduate School
of Library and Information Science; James R. Lawler,
Dalhousie University; Stephen Werner, University of
California, Los Angeles; Rev. Alfred L. Morisette,
S.J. and Berniece Owen, Gonzaga University; and
especially Elizabeth Eisenbach, UCLA Graduate School
of Library and Information Science, whose suggestions on both style and substance were extremely
valuable.   The author thanks them all for their
comments and encouragement.

A special word of thanks must go to Mary Carr,
Gonzaga University, whose unflagging enthusiasm
during the inevitably boring process of style and
copy editing was a constant morale booster.

PREFACE

Librarians are acutely aware of the need to educate students in the use of the library, and there are several suitable general guides such as Robert Downs's and Clara Keller's How to Do Library Research (2nd ed.; Urbana: University of Illinois Press, 1975). While such guides are adequate for the "lower division" undergraduate, there are some librarians who believe that the "upper division" undergraduate and the graduate student will learn more about effective use of the library and its resources when such study is related directly to the student's subject (i.e., "major") interest; this is the raison d'être for such subject-oriented guides as F. N. McCoy's Researching and Writing in History (Berkeley: University of California Press, 1974).

All too frequently, the student is likely to rely upon a very limited number of reference sources in the library purely out of habit. The complexity of the library and its tools tends to foster this behavior pattern. Only when there are glaring inadequacies in a student's term papers are professors likely to mention specialized bibliographies (or dictionaries, encyclopedias, etc.)--hardly a systematic approach to a complex area of study. This

work has been written in recognition of the neces-
sity of introducing to the student of French literature those standard reference sources which are
essential to the acquisition of scholarly competence.

It should be noted here that this book is only
an introduction to library researching: generally,
the titles in Chapter 2 have appeared in Constance
M. Winchell's Guide to Reference Books (8th edition;
Chicago: American Library Association, 1967) and
its supplements, or have been favorably reviewed in
Choice. Given the standard acceptance of these
two reviewing media, the titles included in Chapter
2 would be prime candidates for acquisition by the
medium- to large-sized college or university library.

The bibliographically aware will immediately
note that some titles (e.g., Harrap's New Standard
French and English Dictionary, or Lanson's Histoire
de la littérature française) are likely to be found
in almost any academic library, while others (e.g.,
Wartburg's Französisches etymologisches Wörterbuch,
or the Congrégation de Saint Maur's Histoire
littéraire de la France) will probably only be found
in the largest of the research libraries. Such
seemingly disparate titles are meant to offer a
choice to students and also to indicate the variety
of tools available in the library. It should be
obvious that because of its selectivity, Chapter 2
cannot be considered to be a true bibliographic
guide.

The scope of this work has been consciously
limited to a survey of those tools primarily devoted
to French literature, and has excluded from its pur-

view such fields as linguistics and cinema, which
form part of the broader area of French studies.
This explains the inclusion of subject headings in
each section of the second chapter. They should
suggest to the student that just as there is a certain organization to the bibliographic control of
French literature (with many other possibilities),
so too are there similar tools in other related
fields. By systematically approaching the library
with an adequate understanding of that institution's
limitations and strengths, the student has few
restrictions on the amount of information that can
be accessed.

The ultimate test of this book is the student's
heightened awareness of the wealth and variety of
resources available in the library; its measure of
success lies in educating the French major to become a confident information seeker and a competent
library researcher.

INTRODUCTION

As a student of French literature, you have
something in common with students majoring in
sociology, theater arts, English, anthropology, and
the other social sciences and humanities: an innate
distrust and fear of libraries, reference rooms,
and term paper research. Eminently understandable,
but also curable. You do receive some counsel from
professors and reference librarians, but all too
frequently, the advice comes too late to be of
great usefulness. "You should have consulted ·
French XX." "Haven't you ever heard of Est-ce à
ou de?" "Didn't you know that our library has a
divided catalog?"

Almost every student experiences bewilderment
when such questions are asked. "No, I've never
heard of Est-ce à ou de?, and what is French XX?"
Let us be honest: we all share some of the blame
for this bewilderment. You probably could have
found some extra time to get to know the library;
your professors and the campus librarians probably
could have provided you with a more systematic
introduction to the library, its resources, and
ways to conduct effective library research.

So much for recriminations--we're all over-

1

worked, and it _is_ difficult to find that "extra
time." Let us admit that osmosis and trial and
error are probably not the most efficient ways to
learn about library research. Let us also admit
that you have certain specialized information needs:
you read Montaigne or Molière in preparation for an
explication de texte, and so you need some kind of
dictionary which will explain the denotations and
connotations of words which were current in the
Renaissance or seventeenth century; you have just
begun to study a period of literature or a literary
figure with whom you are unfamiliar, and so you
will need an encyclopedic or biographical source,
or perhaps even a history, to provide you with that
initial overview so necessary to perspective; your
professor has just mentioned a new and important
study on Sartre and politics, but you missed the
citation, and so you need to consult the French
trade or national bibliographies. You might, of
course, be able to determine on your own which
reference works would best answer these questions,
but it is unlikely. Libraries are becoming more
complex and increasingly difficult to use. Osmosis
is just not systematic enough to insure that you
can find answers to those short "ready reference"
questions; nor can it prepare you to cope with the
demands posed by the anxiety-producing term paper
situation.

Ergo, an Introduction to Library Research in
French Literature. It is designed to introduce you
to the ins and outs of using the library, to some
of the reference tools available to help you improve
your skills as a researcher, and to some practical
considerations on how to best use your limited time

2

when you must begin to work on a term paper.
Besides serving as a substitute for the trial and
error method used by many students in getting acquainted with their library and its resources, this
book is based on a fundamentally pragmatic consideration: time. There never seems to be enough
time to read that extra article on Voltaire, to
look up that "important secondary source" for your
study of Mallarmé, to rewrite that awkward third
paragraph in your term paper on Huysmans. While
it is impossible to lengthen the academic term,
a sense of sophistication and confidence in your
ability to use the tools of scholarship is likely
to increase your efficiency as a researcher, and
may even raise your term paper grades.

There is another pragmatic consideration:
your professors usually assume that as your knowledge of French literature increases, so too will
your knowledge of the bibliographic apparatus of
the field. Just as they expect you to strive for
clarity and precision in thought and expression,
so too do they expect you to refine these attri-
butes in your research techniques. They expect
you to not only find answers, but also to formulate
intelligent questions. The acquisition of these
competencies will be considerably facilitated by
a knowledge of the library and its resources.

So welcome to the complex, frustrating, and
rewarding world of libraries, catalogs, bibliographies, dictionaries, and library research. There
are literally hundreds of resources available to
you; take the time now to learn how to use them,
and your labors will be rewarded a hundred times
over later!

1 USING THE LIBRARY EFFECTIVELY

Your college library is an information center
with collections designed to meet both the curricu-
lar and research needs of students and faculty.
From the collection of several hundred thousand
volumes in the average college to the collection of
several million volumes in the largest university,
the library is the heart of any center of learning
and research. Indeed, the quality of a particular
library's collections is almost as important to the
prominence of a college or university as is the
caliber of its faculty.

Since the library is central to any research
you intend to conduct, you need to become acquainted
with some of the characteristics common to almost
all modern American libraries. As you read this
chapter, keep in mind that most of the information
presented here is necessarily general in character,
and that each library makes its own decisions as to
mode of reference service, depth of cataloging,
classification system, and interlibrary loan policy.
Most libraries publish informational pamphlets and
conduct tours, both of which are designed to ac-
quaint you with that individual library's particular idiosyncracies. If you have not previously

5

availed yourself of these services, you should do so after you have studied this chapter.

THE CATALOG

Just as the library is the heart of the modern university, so too is the catalog the heart of the library. In order to use your library effectively, you must have some idea of what you can expect to find in the catalog. Reduced to the simplest possible terms, the catalog is very similar to the index of a book. The index of a book reveals the intellectual content of the publication by citing names and ideas mentioned therein. The catalog describes both the physical and intellectual contents of your library's collections, but unlike the index, it does not necessarily use the terminology found in the individual publications. This explains why many library users experience considerable difficulty in using the catalog.

While there are various types of catalogs, the most common catalog in existence in the United States is the card catalog in dictionary arrangement. In this "dictionary catalog," you will find author, title, and subject cards interfiled in one alphabetical arrangement. (The "divided catalog" is a popular variant of the dictionary catalog in which author and title cards are physically separated from the subject cards.) In many libraries, book and microfilm catalogs, and "on-line" computer terminals are gradually replacing the card catalog, but regardless of mode, any catalog will contain virtually the same kinds of information about the library's collections. Thus, while we will address the features of the "dictionary catalog" in this chapter, almost all of the information is equally applicable to the other kinds of catalogs mentioned above.

The Main Entry Card

Let us begin our discussion of the dictionary catalog, your library's "index," by examining its basic unit: a main entry card for a book. You may have heard the term "main entry" used in the library, but what exactly does it mean? The main entry for a work is its basic access point in the catalog, very often the author card, and it sometimes contains the greatest amount of information about the publication in question. A good general rule of thumb for deciding on main entry is as follows: if there are three authors or less, the main entry will be made under the name of the person named first on the title page. Where authorship responsibility is divided among more than three persons, main entry will be made under the title of the work. Knowing this is important because some of the bibliographic tools which we will discuss later (such as the printed catalogs of the Bibliothèque nationale and the Library of Congress) are "single entry" catalogs--there is only one entry, the "main entry." Remember too that not only people are authors; organizations, called by librarians "corporate bodies," can also author a work. A good example of this would be certain publications by the Modern Language Association of America or the Alliance Française.

Knowing exactly where to look for works by an author is not always easy. Librarians spend a good

7

amount of time in choosing one name and one form of the name for use in their catalogs, thereby insuring that all the works of one author are displayed together for you. Suppose, for example, that you are looking for several books by an author who has written most of his works under a pseudonym. Would you look for these books under the author's real name or under his pseudonym? Generally, you should expect to find all the author's works under the name by which he is primarily identified in standard reference sources. Thus, you would expect to find works by Marie-Henri Beyle under his pseudonym, "Stendhal," and indeed you may. But you must also be aware that cataloging rules have changed considerably over the years, and formerly, an author's works were usually entered under his or her real name. So in the case of "Beyle, Marie Henri" versus "Stendhal," it is more likely that all of his works will be found in the "B" drawers. If this sounds complicated, it is. Happily, most libraries will have cross-references from the name not used to the name chosen for use in the catalog.

The example of "real name" versus "pseudonym" illustrates the problem of choice of name. But what is meant by choice of the "form of the name?" This refers to the problem of picking the form of name for authors with complicated surnames. Where, for example, would you expect to find works by François de Salignac de la Mothe-Fénelon? As with choice of name, the answer to this question depends on how the author is cited in standard reference sources. The preferred form of the name in French in this case is "Fénelon," and so you would look under "Fénelon, François de Salignac de la Mothe-."

There would be cross-references from "Salignac de
la Mothe-Fénelon, François de," and from "Mothe-
Fénelon, François de Salignac de la." Thus, you
will not find Fénelon's works separated in the
catalog, or in other reference sources, in the
"S's," the "M's," and the "F's."

If you are having trouble finding the works of
some author in the catalog, always seek assistance
from a reference librarian who will be able to
ascertain what name is being used.

Take a look now at the main entry card in
Figure 1 on the following page. Jean-Paul Sartre
is the author, and this card serves as the main
entry in the library's catalog. You will notice
that a beginning life date has been added to what
librarians call the "heading" (so called because
it "heads up" or begins the description of the
publication). Life dates are normally added to
author headings when they are easily ascertainable
or when they are needed to distinguish two persons
with the same name. Imagine how many John or Mary
Smiths have written books and how useful such dates
can be in your searching!

Following the main entry heading is a description of the publication beginning with the title
of the book as it appears on the title page.
Occasionally, librarians make use of a device called
"uniform title" in order to bring translations,
editions, or adaptations of a work together in the
catalog with the original work. On the Sartre
main entry card, for example, the "uniform title"--
the title of the original edition of the work--
would have been interposed between the main entry
heading and the translated title and printed in

9

Figure 1

A MAIN ENTRY CARD FOR A BOOK

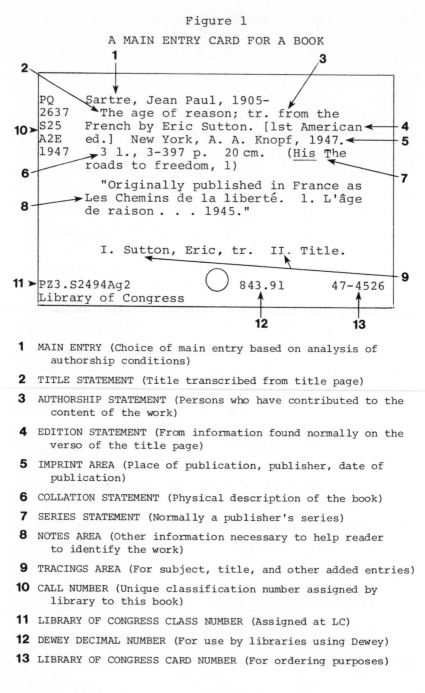

1 MAIN ENTRY (Choice of main entry based on analysis of
  authorship conditions)

2 TITLE STATEMENT (Title transcribed from title page)

3 AUTHORSHIP STATEMENT (Persons who have contributed to the
  content of the work)

4 EDITION STATEMENT (From information found normally on the
  verso of the title page)

5 IMPRINT AREA (Place of publication, publisher, date of
  publication)

6 COLLATION STATEMENT (Physical description of the book)

7 SERIES STATEMENT (Normally a publisher's series)

8 NOTES AREA (Other information necessary to help reader
  to identify the work)

9 TRACINGS AREA (For subject, title, and other added entries)

10 CALL NUMBER (Unique classification number assigned by
   library to this book)

11 LIBRARY OF CONGRESS CLASS NUMBER (Assigned at LC)

12 DEWEY DECIMAL NUMBER (For use by libraries using Dewey)

13 LIBRARY OF CONGRESS CARD NUMBER (For ordering purposes)

10

brackets in the following manner:

Sartre, Jean Paul, 1905-

[L'âge de raison]

The age of reason; . . .

This would insure that all of the translations of
this novel, regardless of language or choice of
title, would be displayed together behind the original edition in the catalog. When a library <u>does</u>
make use of "uniform title," it is usually for very
prolific authors, such as Voltaire or Shakespeare,
and you will generally find references from the
variant title to the original "uniform" title.

Another important part of the description is
the authorship statement. Obviously, this is a
work <u>by</u> Sartre, but it has been translated by Eric
Sutton. There may be various other translations or
editions. While the Sutton translation of Sartre's
<u>L'âge de raison</u> is very probably a reputable one,
there are certainly many translations of many works
which might not be as reliable. As you become
better versed in the conventions of academia, the
statement of authorship will become increasingly
important to you. Is the editor well known? How
about the illustrator, translator, or compiler?
Knowing the names of persons associated with the
publication of a particular work may be an important criterion for selection.

Another element of the description is the
edition statement, which may or may not be present
depending upon the particular publication in hand.
An "edition" refers to all the copies of a particular work produced from a single setting of type, and
is thus not synonymous with the term "printing."

11

For the Sartre work, the catalog card tells us that
we have the "1st American ed." It could just as
easily have been the "1st British ed." or the
"Complete unexpurgated ed." The edition statement
will be important to you when currency of information is necessary. If, for example, you are looking
for a glossary of literary terms and you have a
choice between the "1st ed." and the "2nd revised
ed.", you will almost certainly choose the latter
edition since the definitions contained therein
are more likely to be up-to-date.

Following the edition statement, you will find
what librarians call the "imprint." This includes
the place of publication, the name of the publisher,
and the date of publication (or perhaps the copyright date). Had the librarian been unable to ascertain this information, the publisher statement
might have read "[n.p., n.d.]" (no place, no date),
or, under the latest rules for the cataloging of
books, "[s.l. : s.n.]" meaning sine loco (no place)
and sine nomine (no name).

An important part of the description of a book
is what is termed the "collation." Here the librarian describes for you the book as a physical
object. In our case, the book is composed of three
leaves followed by pages numbered from three to
three hundred ninety-seven. The book is twenty
centimeters high (height is always given in centimeters; librarians anticipated metric conversion by
several decades!). While this may not seem greatly
useful at first glance, consider some of the other
possibilities for collation. If you had two translations of Sartre's L'âge de raison, both translated by Sutton, but with the following collations,

which would you choose?

3 ℓ., 3-397 p.   20 cm.

xx, 553 p. front., ports., illus. (some col.)   36 cm.

The second book is obviously larger than the first,
with frontispiece, portraits, and other illustrations (some in color); it contains twenty preliminary pages numbered in roman numerals with
553 pages of text following that; it stands sixteen centimeters higher than the first book.
Again, which would you choose? Your answer will
depend upon your particular need at the moment.
If you are looking for a reading copy of the novel
as part of a rather hurried assignment for a class,
you are certainly more likely to want the smaller,
more portable version. If, on the other hand, you
are interested in leisurely perusing a larger
illustrated book, the second publication may be more
suitable.

The statement in parentheses following the
collation is called the "series statement." In
this case, The Age of Reason is the first part of
the author's series The Roads to Freedom. Often,
however, the "series" is a publisher's series such
as Seghers's "Poètes d'aujourd'hui." Again, this
part of the description serves to help you identify
this particular version of this particular work,
and if you have been favorably impressed with
another volume in a certain publisher's series, the
series statement could be a deciding factor in your
choice of one publication over another.

Separated from the main body of the description on a catalog card is the "notes area." On our
Sartre main entry card, the librarian has taken a

13

quote from the publication which will explain this individual book's relationship to other versions and editions of the work. The "notes area" is also used to detail the contents of a particular work (usually a multi-volume work), to explain certain other features of the physical volume or of the intellectual content, to clarify information presented in the formal part of the description, and often to indicate whether or not a bibliography, bibliographical footnotes, or an index are included in the book. (Books with bibliographies and indexes will generally be easier to use than those without them.)

Below the "notes area" are two "added entries"--extra access points in the catalog--both preceded by roman numerals. Since The Age of Reason is a work of fiction, there are no subject entries, which would have been preceded by arabic numerals, and so we have only two added entries for this book: one under the translator's name, and one under the title of the translation. Normally, copies of the main entry card are reproduced and then the added entry headings (in our case, "Sutton, Eric, Tr." and "The Age of reason") will be typed above the main entry heading for filing in the card catalog. Thus, we have three access points for this Sartre novel in the catalog. Other possible non-subject added entries could include those for joint authors, editors, compilers, illustrators (if the illustrations are an important part of the work), and series. These kinds of added entries, subject entries, and the main entry, are the principal access points under which you might expect to find a particular publication in your library's catalog.

The information presented thus far applies generally to books cataloged prior to 1974. Since that time, books have been cataloged under slightly different rules, and with a slightly different format as illustrated in Figure 2. While this new,

---

Figure 2

EXAMPLE OF DESCRIPTIVE CATALOGING IN ISBD-M FORMAT

Sartre, Jean Paul, 1905-
    The age of reason / Jean-Paul Sartre ; translated from the French by Eric Sutton. -- 1st American ed. -- New York : Knopf, 1947.
    3 leaves, 3-397 p. ; 20 cm. -- (<u>His</u> The roads to freedom ; 1)

---

internationally acceptable format is probably not confusing, do not hesitate to confer with a reference librarian if you have difficulty in interpreting a particular catalog record. Remember too that many cataloging practices have changed considerably over the years, thus creating inconsistencies in the catalogs of many libraries. Such inconsistencies--librarians call them headaches-- can be explained by your reference librarian.

Classification

Assuming that your library is an "open stack" collection where library users freely enter, browse, and choose their own books, the majority of the library's materials will have been classified so as to produce a useful shelf arrangement wherein books on chemistry are not interspersed with books on literature. Classification is really nothing but

15

Figure 3

LIBRARY OF CONGRESS CLASSIFICATION

A	General works
B-BJ	Philosophy. Psychology
BL-BX	Religion
C	Auxiliary Science of History
D	History: General and Old World (Eastern Hemisphere)
E-F	History: America (Western Hemisphere)
G	Geography. Anthropology. Recreation
H	Social Sciences
J	Political Science
K	Law. Philosophy of Law
KD	Law of the United Kingdom and Ireland
KF	Law of the United States
L	Education
M	Music. Books on Music
N	Fine Arts
P-PA	General Philology and Linguistics. Classical Languages and Literatures
PA Suppl.	Byzantine and Modern Greek Literature. Medieval and Modern Latin Literature
PB-PH	Modern European Languages
PG	Russian Literature
PJ-PM	Languages and Literatures of Asia, Africa, Oceania. American Indian Languages. Artificial Languages
P-PM Suppl.	Index to Languages and Dialects
PN, PR, PS, PZ	General Literature. English and American Literature. Fiction in English. Juvenile Literature
PQ, Part 1	French Literature
PQ, Part 2	Italian, Spanish, and Portuguese Literatures
PT, Part 1	German Literature
PT, Part 2	Dutch and Scandinavian Literatures
Q	Science
R	Medicine
S	Agriculture
T	Technology
U	Military Science
V	Naval Science
Z	Bibliography. Library Science

a kind of shorthand notation which describes the subject or form of a work and gives each publication an "address" on the library's shelves. The two most common classification systems in use in the United States are the Library of Congress Classification (LC) and the Dewey Decimal Classification (Dewey, or DDC). In recent years, more and more college and university libraries have been reclassifying their collections from Dewey to LC, while most public libraries use Dewey.

On the main entry card in Figure 1, you will have noted three different classification numbers. The one in the upper left hand corner and the one in the lower left hand side of the card are both Library of Congress numbers; the number slightly to the right of the center of the card is a Dewey number. Let us first examine the LC numbers. These "numbers" are composed first of a letter (or letters) to indicate the main class (see Figure 3), and then numbers to indicate the particular subject or form within a class. The "numbers" may then be further subdivided by other combinations of letters and numbers to form a complete "call number" or address for the particular publication. For example, the Library of Congress assigned our Sutton translation the number "PZ3.S2494Ag2." The "PZ3" is their number for "Fiction in English (including translations)"; the "S2494" is a number which represents the author (Sartre); and the "Ag2" represents the title of the work (Age of reason). The catalogers at the Library of Congress have thus made one suggestion to libraries for the classification of this book, but their answer is clearly not the only one when

Figure 4

LIBRARY OF CONGRESS CLASSIFICATION:
FRENCH LITERATURE

PQ	History and Criticism
1-150	General
151-221	Medieval
226-307	Modern
400-491	Poetry
500-591	Drama
601-771	Prose and prose fiction
781-841	Folk Literature (including texts)
	Collections
1101-1141	General
1161-1193	Poetry
1211-1241	Drama
1243-1297	Prose
	Old French Literature (to ca. 1500/50)
1300-1391	Collections
	Individual Authors and Works
1411-1545	To 1350/1400
1551-1595	(14th-) 15th Century (to ca. 1525)
	Modern Literature
	Individual Authors
1600-1709	16th Century
1710-1935	17th Century
1947-2147	18th Century
2149-2551	19th Century
2600-2651	20th Century
3801-3999	Provincial, Local, Colonial, etc.

you examine the classification number assigned in "our" library: "PQ2637.S25A2E 1947." This "PQ" number represents individual French authors in the 20th century, with a number for Sartre, ".S25," and for the title, "A2," and an "E" denoting that this is an English translation. The date has been added so as to distinguish this "1st American ed." from any subsequent editions which may be acquired by the library. Obviously, "our" library has decided that its patrons would prefer to find all editions and translations of L'âge de raison shelved together in the stacks with the original editions which was assigned the number "PQ2637."

The individual classification schedules at the Library of Congress have been designed by subject specialists to create the most useful shelf arrangement for other specialists in their field. The efforts of specialists in French literature are displayed in Figure 4 which outlines that section of the "PQ" class devoted to French literature.

You may already be familiar with the Dewey Decimal System (see Figure 5 on the following pages). It is a numerical classification scheme using a "base number" of three digits. To these three digit numbers will be added other numbers which will fully express the subject content. Notice the breakdown of numbers within the decimal range "840" for French literature in Figure 6 on page 21; here the form of the work is of primary importance, as opposed to the LC system in which period is of equal importance. To these "base numbers" in "840" will be added numbers from a separate table entitled "Subdivisions of individual

19

Figure 5

DEWEY DECIMAL DIVISIONS

000 GENERAL WORKS

  010 Bibliography
  020 Library Science
  030 General Encyclopedias
  040 General Collected Essays
  050 General Periodicals
  060 General Societies, Museums
  070 Journalism
  080 Collected Works
  090 Book Rarities

100 PHILOSOPHY

  110 Metaphysics
  120 Metaphysical Theories
  130 Branches of Psychology
  140 Philosophic System
  150 Psychology
  160 Logic
  170 Ethics
  180 Ancient Philosophy
  190 Modern Philosophy

200 RELIGION

  210 Natural Religion
  220 Bible
  230 Doctrinal Theology
  240 Practical Theology
  250 Pastoral Theology
  260 Ecclasiastical Theology
  270 Christian Churches History
  280 Christian Churches & Sects
  290 Non-Christian Religions

300 SOCIAL SCIENCES

  310 Statistics
  320 Political Science
  330 Economics
  340 Law
  350 Public Administration
  360 Social Welfare
  370 Education
  380 Commerce
  390 Customs

400 PHILOLOGY

  410 Comparative Philology
  420 English Language
  430 German
  440 French
  450 Italian
  460 Spanish
  470 Latin
  480 Greek
  490 Other Languages

500 PURE SCIENCE

  510 Mathematics
  520 Astronomy
  530 Physics
  540 Chemistry
  550 Earth Sciences
  560 Paleontology
  570 Biological Sciences
  580 Botany
  590 Zoology

600 APPLIED SCIENCES

  610 Medicine
  620 Engineering
  630 Agriculture
  640 Home Economics
  650 Business
  660 Industrial Chemistry
  670 Manufacturing
  680 Mechanic Trades
  690 Building

700 ARTS & RECREATION

  710 Landscape/Civic Art
  720 Architecture
  730 Sculpture
  740 Drawing
  750 Painting
  760 Prints & Print Making
  770 Photography
  780 Music
  790 Recreation

800 LITERATURE	900 HISTORY
810 American Literature	910 Geography & Travel
820 English Literature	920 Collective Biography
830 German Literature	930 Ancient History
840 French Literature	940 History of Europe
850 Italian Literature	950 Asia
860 Spanish Literature	960 Africa
870 Latin Literature	970 North America
880 Greek Literature	980 South America
890 Other Literatures	990 Oceania & Polar Regions

literatures" to form a full classification number. For example, the number "08035" appears in this table under the heading "Collections dealing with specific themes and subjects: Humanity and human existence." The Dewey number "846.08035" would thus signal a collection of French letters on this topic. The number assigned to the Sartre novel, "843.91," indicates French fiction ("843") of the twentieth century (".91"). A full call number would probably also include numbers for author and/or title, and the date of the publication.

Figure 6

DEWEY DECIMAL NUMBERS IN FRENCH LITERATURE

840   Literatures of Romance Languages

841   French Poetry
842   French Drama
843   French Fiction
844   French Essays
845   French Speeches
846   French Letters
847   French Satire & Humor
848   French Miscellaneous Writings
849   Provençal & Catalan

An important feature of both classification
systems is that they classify by subject or form.
Sartre's L'âge de raison is a novel and will be
classed in "PQ" for LC and "843" for Dewey; any of
his philosophical tracts such as Critique de la
raison dialectique will be classed in "B" (LC)
and "190" (Dewey). Thus, all of Sartre's works
will be displayed together in the catalog, but
they will not be shelved together in the stacks.
If you are a browser, you will need to make judicious use of the information presented in Figures
4 and 6 when browsing through the stacks. To be
safe, make a practice of browsing through the
catalog as well as the stacks.[1]

Before you go to the stacks to find a particular book or periodical, make sure that you have
copied down the full call number as well as any
special location indicators, such as those for books
in the reference department, the rare book room,
etc., or symbols indicating that the book is over-
sized. Remember too that the author and title
numbers we have mentioned are decimal integers.
Thus, you will find PQ2637.S2499A2E 1947 before
PQ2637.S25A2E 1947 because .S2499 is smaller
than .S25.

Subject Headings

So far we have only addressed the problem of
"accessing" information in the catalog by main
entry or "non-subject" added entry such as title,
editor, etc. This is important to you when you are
looking for a particular publication. But you also
come to the catalog wanting to know what the library has on a given subject, and it is here that

you may encounter problems with what may librarians refer to as "vocabulary control." Where, for example, will you look in the catalog for materials on women authors in France? In the "A" drawer for "Authors, Women" or "Authors, Female"; in the "F" drawer for "Female authors" or "France--Women authors"; or in the "W" drawer for "Women authors?" You have a pretty good idea of what you want, but does your "vocabulary" coincide with that used in the library catalog?

Chances are good that your library uses the latest edition of the Library of Congress Subject Headings (now in its 8th edition, 1975, and commonly referred to as LCSH). The LCSH lists subject headings which may be used in a library catalog, and is often available for public use in the reference area or near the catalog in many libraries. In general, the most specific subject headings will be assigned to library materials; this principle of "specificity" means that you would not expect to find information about women authors in France under the broader heading "Authors." Were you to consult the latest edition of LCSH, you would find the subject heading displayed in Figure 7 on page 24.

This excerpt from LCSH conveys some useful information. The word "Direct" following the subject heading refers to what librarians call "method of geographical subdivision." If, for example, the subject "Women authors" is dealt with in terms of a specific place, you will find this indicated by a direct subdivision such as "Women authors--Paris" or "Women authors--San Francisco (City)" in the catalog. Had the subject heading been followed by the word "Indirect," this would have meant that

Figure 7
A LIBRARY OF CONGRESS SUBJECT HEADING

WOMEN AUTHORS (Direct)   (PN 471-9)

Here are entered works on the attainments of women as authors. Collections of works written by women are entered under Women's writings. Collections of works written about women are entered under Woman--Literary collections. Works which discuss the representation of women in literature are entered under Women in literature.

    sa   Women dramatists
         Women journalists
         Women novelists
         Women poets
     x   Authors, Women
         Women as authors
    xx   Authors
         Authorship

Notes under Woman--Literary collections; Women in literature; Women's writings--Biography.

---

specific place names (cities, towns, etc.) would have been entered indirectly after the larger geographical unit (e.g., "Women authors--France--Paris," or "Women authors--California--San Francisco (City)"). Following the statement "Direct" is an indication of where most works on this subject will be classified using LC. Materials dealing with the subject "Women authors" would be found in the stack range PN 471-479. If your library's collections are classified using the LC scheme, you may use this information for browsing in the stacks.

Beneath the subject heading is a "scope note" which tells you what kinds of works should receive this heading. It will help you to narrow or broaden your subject search--did you really want "works on the attainments of women as authors," or would the subject heading "Women's writings" be more specific? There are also other suggestions below the "scope note." The designation "sa" means that at the subject heading "Women authors" you may find a note in the catalog telling you to "See also Women dramatists, etc."[2] Notice that these are narrower related headings. The designation "x" means that the two headings "Authors, Women" and "Women as authors" are not used in the catalog; there will be "see" references from these headings to "Women authors." The designation "xx" indicates two broader related headings; "see also" references will appear in the catalog from these headings to "Women authors." The final lines of the subject heading tell us that the "scope note" will also appear in the catalog under these other headings.

Is this the only place in the catalog where you will find materials on "Women authors?" Not at all. You will also find important material under the names of individual women authors such as George Sand. LCSH does not, of course, list proper names, but it does indicate typical subdivisions which could be used under an author's name. The example is William Shakespeare, and some of the subdivisions include:

--Adaptations	--Biography
--Allusions	--Concordances

--Anniversaries	--Criticism, Textual
(Subdivided by Date)	
--Authorship	--Ethical ideas
--Autographs	--Technique
--Bibliography	--Translations

Knowing that a subject heading can have many possible subdivisions will be particularly important to you when you are looking for materials on a prominent author about whom much has been written (e.g., Voltaire).

Serials

So far, we have only addressed the cataloging of books. But books are not the only materials collected by libraries. Much of the information you need most will be found in serials. A "serial," in library jargon, is the generic term for those publications which are issued in successive parts at intervals (usually _regular_ intervals) and intended to be continued indefinitely. Serials thus include periodicals, newspapers, annuals, numbered monographic series, and the proceedings and transactions of societies.

Serials, because they are normally composed of individual contributions by various authors, are usually entered in the catalog under their _title_. Thus, the main entry cards for the journals _Tel quel_ or _Revue d'histoire littéraire de la France_ will be found in the "T" and "R" drawers respectively. Some serials, however, contain the name of the organization which issues them as a part of the title. In these cases, the main entry will be made under the name of the organization. This is the case for the journal _PMLA_ (see Figure 8)

26

Figure 8

A MAIN ENTRY CARD FOR A SERIAL

```
PB      Modern Language Association of America.
6           Publications.  v.1-
M72     1884/85-
        Menasha, Wisc.  [etc.]
             v. in      23-25 cm.

        At head of title:  PMLA.
        Vols. 8-35 called also new ser. v.1-28.
        Title varies:  1884/85, Transactions;
        1886-87, Transactions and proceedings.
        Cover title, 1929-     , PMLA.

          1. Philology, Modern.  I. Title: PMLA.
```

which was entered by the Library of Congress under
the Modern Language Association of America.

As you can see from the main entry card, the
description of a serial reflects its peculiar publication pattern. The PMLA is issued in volumes
(v.1-   ) and began publication with its 1884/85
issue. When this journal someday ceases publication, these "open entries" will be "closed." For
example, were the PMLA to see its final issue in
1980, the library would fill in the ending volume
number (v.1-100) and the ending date (1884/85-1980).
Since the library may bind more than one volume
together, the "collation" would be filled in to
read "100 v. in 88," or something to that effect.

Serials are generally the most difficult publications to identify and cite bibliographically. The notes on the PMLA card indicate one of the principal reasons for this: changes in title. Also, organizations may frequently change their names to emphasize a new focal point for their activities; they may change the volume numbering; they may cease publication of their periodical only to reinstate it six months later under a slightly different title (e.g., Proceedings and Transactions of the . . . becoming Transactions and Proceedings of the . . .). Make things easy on yourself by coming to the catalog with a full and accurate citation: author and title of the article, full name of the periodical, volume, dates (if any), number (if any), and pages. Remember also to check behind the serial main entry card for "holdings statement" cards which many libraries use to check off the volume numbers owned by the library. There is little point in running upstairs to find your article if the particular volume or number in which it appeared was never acquired by your library.

Filing

There is a final area which is vitally important to your understanding of the structure of the catalog: filing. The filing standard for most libraries in the United States is the American Library Association's ALA Rules for Filing Catalog Cards (2nd ed.; Chicago: American Library Association, 1968). According to this work, the basic order is alphabetical, word by word, with alphabetizing letter by letter within a word. In most libraries, the English language alphabet is the standard used for alphabetizing, and so foreign

languages and English are interfiled, with dia-
critical marks ignored in most cases (e.g., "è" or
"é" will interfile with "e").

You have already seen that there are several
different kinds of entries to be found in the
catalog: main entries, title entries, and subject
entries, to name just three. Given the basic rule
for alphabetizing, there is an additional method of
arrangement for "author headings." The following
rules from the ALA Rules (Rule 26A, p. 114) will
help you to understand the arrangement of the
Sartre "file" in Figure 9:

> Under an author heading arrange different
> kinds of entries in groups in the following
> order:
> 1) Works by the author, subarranged alpha-
>   betically by their titles
> 2) Works about the author, without sub-
>   division, subarranged alphabetically by
>   their main entries; except subject en-
>   tries for individual works, which are
>   arranged in group 1 immediately after the
>   author entries for the same work [. . .]
> 3) Works about the author, with subdivision,
>   subarranged alphabetically by the sub-
>   divisions.

Take a look now at Figure 9 on the following
page, and notice that in cards one and three,
Sartre is a "joint author" and so the file is subarranged by the titles of the works, and not by
the main entries (Nizan and Rebeyrolle). In cards
two and four, you will notice that the initial articles ("L'" and "The"), regardless of language, are

29

Figure 9

FILING ARRANGEMENT

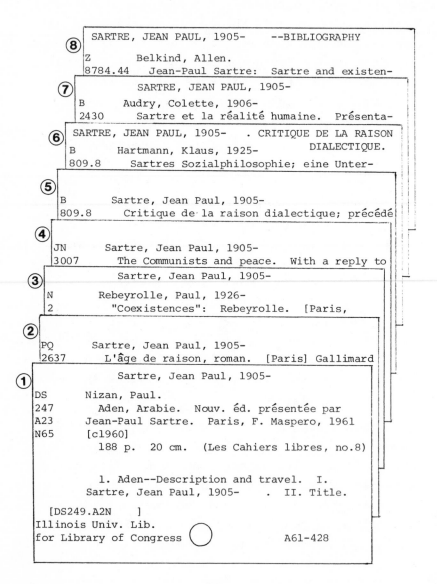

ignored in filing, except, of course, in the case
of _personal names_ such as La Fontaine. Card six
exemplifies the exception to rule two, that a subject entry for an individual work will file _imme-
diately_ after that work. Cards six through eight
are all subject-entry cards, and the subject
headings will probably be typed in upper-case
letters or in red. Any title cards that begin with
Sartre's name (e.g., the title in card seven) would
file _after_ the subject cards.

Sometimes, when an author was particularly
prolific, or his or her critics quite voluminous,
a library may make use of another arrangement. Such
is the case with Voltaire, where the arrangement
might be as follows:

> Complete works
> Correspondence
> Individual titles
>> Candide
>> Henriade
>> Mahomet
>> La Pucelle d'Orléans
> Subjects
> Titles

Such an arrangement can be extremely helpful in
those situations where cards for an author may
occupy one, two, or even three drawers in the
catalog. In such cases where filing differs from
the norm, you will sometimes find "guide cards" in
the catalog explaining the exceptional filing
arrangement.

While much more could be said about filing
(the _ALA Rules_ cover over two hundred pages), the

31

foregoing discussion suffices to give you an idea
of some of the difficulties you could encounter
when using the catalog. Check near your library's
card catalog for any instructions which the librarians may have posted to explain their filing
arrangement, and in case of doubt, consult a
reference librarian.

INTERLIBRARY LOANS

The college and university library does not
receive the kind of financial support now that it
did in the 1960s, and in every department certain
economies are being implemented. The huge book
budgets of the earlier decades have greatly dimin-
ished, and libraries are now looking toward the
"library network" concept in an effort to avoid the
duplication of costly, specialized, and little-used
materials. Such materials will now probably be
acquired by only the largest of the research libraries.

Since no library can possibly hope to collect
every book or periodical you might need, there is
an important service offered to graduate students,
faculty, and sometimes to undergraduate students:
the interlibrary loan. Through this service, your
campus library locates materials which it does not
have, and which you need, at another library, and
borrows or obtains a photocopy of those materials.
Often, a librarian will ask you to fill out forms
similar to those in Figure 10 on the following page.
Using the information you provide, an interlibrary
loans librarian will first verify that your library
does not have the materials; he or she will then
verify that the materials do exist, and then locate

Figure 10

INTERLIBRARY LOAN REQUEST FORMS

BOOK REQUEST (Type or print plainly; no abbreviations)

AUTHOR _Barbéris, Pierre_
      Last name   First names

TITLE _Le monde de Balzac_

PLACE OF
PUB. _Paris_   PUBLISHER _Arthaud_   DATE OF PUB. _1973_

PRINTED SOURCE OF
REFERENCE _MLA Int'l Bibliography, vol. 2, 1973, p. 35_
    (Include vol. if any, date of pub., page no., etc.)
==
BORROWER _John T. Day_   STATUS _Undergrad-_

ADDRESS _383 Campus Drive, San Francisco, CA 94743_

DEPT. _French_   LAST USABLE DATE _1-30-79_

PERIODICAL REQUEST (Type or print plainly; no abbreviations)

PERIODICAL _Rice University Studies_

PLACE OF PUB. _Houston, Texas_ VOL. _59(iii)_ DATE _1973_ PAGES _11-81_

AUTHOR OF ARTICLE _Sobel, Margaret_

TITLE OF ARTICLE _Balzac's Le père Goriot and Dicken's Dombey and Son: A comparison_

PRINTED SOURCE OF
REFERENCE _MLA Int'l Bibliography, Vol. 2, 1973, p. 36_
    (Include vol. if any, date of pub., page no., etc.)
==
BORROWER _John T. Day_   STATUS _Undergrad._

ADDRESS _383 Campus Drive, San Francisco, CA 94743_

DEPT. _French_   LAST USABLE DATE _1-30-79_

33

and request the materials from a library which holds them.[3] The costs for interlibrary loan may be absorbed by your library, or by you, the user.

There are two very important items of information requested on the book and periodical request forms: "Last usable date" and "Printed source of reference." Interlibrary loans can take from four to six weeks (and maybe longer in some cases) to process, and so if you have just started your term paper in week seven of a ten-week quarter (which was poor planning on your part!), it will be far too late in most cases to gather materials using interlibrary loan. Plan ahead for your research, and allow enough time for the arrival of those materials which you may need.

The other item of information requested on the form, "Printed source of reference," asks you to tell the librarian where you found your citation to the book or periodical article you need. When you search through bibliographies and indexes, it would be very desirable for you to annotate your citations with the name and date of the reference work you are using. While this may seem needlessly time-consuming, you will be happy to have spent an extra thirty seconds on each citation so as to avoid a half hour search later trying to remember where you originally found the citation. We will discuss this further in Chapter 3.

THE REFERENCE FUNCTION

Having learned about some of the inevitable pitfalls in using the library and its catalog, you should now become acquainted with your library's reference staff, whose function it is to answer all of those questions which a book such as this one could never hope to do.

One of the reference librarian's most frequent complaints is that students (and faculty, for that matter) hesitate to ask questions. Reference librarians are paid money to answer your questions, so make them earn their salaries! They are at their desks because the library is not by any means an easy tool to use; it is a complex growing organism which only trained professionals and experienced researchers can use with anything approximating total proficiency.

Another oft-cited lament of reference librarians is that library users tend to avoid asking specific questions. It is quite common to hear students asking for books on birds when they actually wanted to know why their parakeet was losing all of its feathers. Always sit down before you start your library searching and ask yourself what you are really looking for. This will not only facilitate your researching in the catalog, periodical indexes, and subject bibliographies, but it will help you to frame your questions more clearly and precisely, thus allowing a reference librarian to serve you more effectively. Remember too that it is perfectly legitimate to approach the reference desk when you have no idea of what you're looking for, or if you're feeling confused about a search strategy you have adopted and which seems to be failing.

In the following chapter, you will learn of the many types of information sources available to expedite your work as a student. But this discussion, like our examination of the library and its

35

central organism, the catalog, is abbreviated and selective in scope. Reference librarians keep an eye out for new publications and have a "feel" for your library's collections, so it is quite likely that they may be able to point you toward a new work which would answer your question very satisfactorily.

NOTES

1. Most libraries have a special catalog called a "shelflist" which lists, in call number order, every publication in the library (just as you would find them on the library shelves). Sometimes, the shelflist is available for public use and is helpful as a browsing tool.

2. Some libraries do not use "See also" references in their catalogs.

3. If you are interested in finding out for yourself whether a library in your area has a particular book, you can turn to the National Union Catalog (discussed in Chapter 2 under "Library Catalogs"). If you need to find a library that has a particular serial, you can turn to the Union List of Serials in Libraries of the United States and Canada and its supplement called New Serial Titles (this latter title appears monthly and cumulates quarterly and annually). Both of these reference tools list serials published throughout the world and held by libraries in North America. Your reference libarian can explain its arrangement.

2 THE MATERIALS OF RESEARCH

Now that you know something about the structure and services of your library, you need to learn
about some of the major information sources you are
likely to find there. In this chapter you will find
information on some of the major reference tools
devoted to French literature: dictionaries, encyclopedias, biographical sources, bibliographies,
dissertations, book reviews, and guides to special
collections. As you read, keep in mind that this
is a selective list which treats French literature
by period and not by genre; for more comprehensive
coverage, you should turn to some of the bibliographic guides mentioned later.

In general, this chapter is arranged as
follows: some remarks about the kinds of uses to
which a type of information source may be put, some
possible subject headings culled from the Library of
Congress Subject Headings for further library
searching, and an alphabetical listing by library
main entry of some typical information sources in
that category, with annotations as to scope,
coverage, and arrangement. Remember that while
most libraries will probably have cataloged the
various titles with the main entry listed here and

with the subject headings from the Library of Congress, there may be significant differences. Take note of them when they occur.

The reference tools listed in this chapter deal primarily with French literature, although there are some tools mentioned that are likely to be useful to any academic library user, such as the guides to special collections, some national library catalogs, etc. For information on other sources that deal with some of the broader areas of French studies (e.g., linguistics, cinema, pedagogy), consult the bibliographic guides listed in this chapter and your library's catalog. If in doubt as to whether or not a tool exists that might be able to answer your question, always consult a reference librarian.

DICTIONARIES

There is perhaps no more important information source for the student of literature than the dictionary, for the life force of any literary genre is the individual word in all of its richness and complexity. Librarians often refer to dictionaries as "word books" because of their great variety in scope and coverage: historical, etymological, slang, synonym, etc. Besides simply defining words, dictionaries may also give examples of pronunciation, variant forms, usage, and synonyms. Dictionaries are said to be descriptive if they just define the word in question; they are prescriptive if they also indicate the appropriateness of the word in a context. Most English language dictionaries are descriptive, while most French language dictionaries are prescriptive.

For other unabridged or abridged dictionaries, check in your library's catalog under either "French language--Dictionaries," or "French language--Terms and phrases."

Unabridged Dictionaries

The unabridged dictionary gives the most complete and detailed definitions of those words considered to comprise the "standard" (i.e., written) language. You will turn to the unabridged dictionary when you need the fullest definition possible. Within this category there are four notable titles:

➤ Académie française, Paris. Dictionnaire de
  l'Académie française. 8. éd. Paris:
  Hachette, 1932-35.

This is a standard work in two volumes, the first edition of which was published in 1694. The Académie française is concerned with the preservation of the linguistic integrity of the French language, and so words are admitted into the great lexicon only after judicious scrutiny. The definitions are clear and concise and are generally accompanied by examples which indicate usage, but the dictionary does not include etymology. The dictionary is considered to be strong in literary language, and many of the greatest French writers are cited. The earlier editions of the Dictionnaire de l'Académie française can be very useful for the study of texts of earlier centuries.

➤ Imbs, Paul, ed. Trésor de la langue française:
  Dictionnaire de la langue du XIXe et du XXe
  siècle (1789-1960). Paris: Editions du

Centre national de la recherche scientifique, 1971- .

The TLF, currently being compiled at the
C.N.R.S. under the direction of Paul Imbs, is
planned to be the ultimate French historical
dictionary and will probably supersede both
the Littré and the Robert (see below) when completed. The plan for the TLF is to issue
several different multi-volume sets, each devoted to a different period of the language.
This first set (1789-1960) draws its language
from 416 texts of the nineteenth century and
586 texts of the twentieth century, and will
include some 70,000 words. Each entry includes
definitions, examples from various literary
and scientific texts, large sections on the
history and etymology of the word, pronunciation, references to books and articles which
contain discussions of the word in question,
a frequency count of occurrences in the texts
examined, and finally, a detailed inventory of
syntax and usage. In volume one, the entry for
the preposition "à" occupies fifteen pages,
with a column-long bibliography! The first
set of the TLF, which is estimated to range
anywhere from fifteen to sixty volumes, will
probably not be complete for many years.[1]

Littré, Emile. Dictionnaire de la langue
    française. Ed. intégrale. Paris: Jean-
    Jacques Pauvert, 1956-58.

This seven-volume dictionary was compiled
late in the nineteenth century. The "édition
intégrale" incorporates the original four
volumes and their supplements into one alpha-

bet "selon les intentions de l'auteur." While
Littré might not be an appropriate choice for
use with a mid-twentieth century author, it
remains important for pre-twentieth century
language, and is filled with quotations. Furthermore, the Littré includes etymology and the
history of word meanings and also notes grammatical usage.

➤ Robert, Paul. Dictionnaire alphabétique et
    analogique de la langue française: Les mots
    et les associations d'idées. Paris:
    Société du Nouveau Littré, 1970-71.

This excellent dictionary in six volumes
serves to update the Littré. It not only gives
the definitions, etymology, and history of
words, but also includes synonyms and antonyms.
The Robert, like the Littré, also cites many
writers from all centuries. You will find the
Robert to be helpful when writing papers because of its many cross-references which should
help you to choose le mot juste.

Abridged (Desk) Dictionaries

An abridged or "desk" dictionary defines fewer
words than its unabridged counterpart and often
drops some of the extra features (examples of usage,
etymology, etc.) found in the larger multi-volume
dictionaries. Because of this, the abridged dictionary is most likely to be useful in "ready-reference" situations or as a portable reading companion.
While almost every major publishing house has a
variety of desk dictionaries available, there are
two important "standard" titles which are frequently
cited:

➤ Larousse, Pierre. Nouveau petit Larousse:
Dictionnaire encyclopédique pour tous.
Paris: Larousse, 1967. (And other re-
printings and editions.)

This Larousse dictionary is divided into
two parts, the first of which gives the definitions, pronunciation, and examples of usage of
words. The second part is a short, alphabetically arranged glossary of proper names
(persons, places, and things) with very brief
annotations. The dictionary is copiously
illustrated.

➤ Robert, Paul. Dictionnaire alphabétique et
analogique de la langue française. 9. éd.
Paris: Société du Nouveau Littré, 1972.
(And other reprintings and editions.)

Known more commonly as the Petit Robert,
this is probably the best desk dictionary for
the advanced undergraduate and graduate student
because of its detailed definitions and
"synonym-antonym" feature. Based upon the
larger seven-volume set, it does not include
either illustrations or biographical and geographical information, but does include etymology, pronunciation, and examples of usage.

Period Dictionaries

Period dictionaries are devoted to documenting
the meanings of words as they existed at various
periods of the development of the language, usually
entering the word as it was originally spelled.
Normally they will be of maximum benefit when you
are engaged in specialized, in-depth studies of particular works, or for general philological purposes.

For other period dictionaries, check in your library's catalog under the subject heading "French language" with the following subdivisions: "--Old French--Dictionaries," "--To 1500--Dictionaries," and "--Early modern, 1500-1700--Dictionaries."

Medieval

➤ Godefroy, Frédéric Eugène. Dictionnaire de l'ancienne langue française, et de tous ses dialectes, du IXe au XVe siècles. . . . Publié sous les auspices du Ministère de l'instruction publique. Paris: Bouillon, 1881-1902. (Reprinted: New York: Kraus Reprint Corp., 1961.)

Because of its expanded period coverage (ninth to fifteenth centuries), Godefroy is often considered to be the "standard" medieval dictionary. It is filled with quotations, examples of usage, and variant spellings. The first eight volumes comprise the basic dictionary, A-Z; volumes nine and ten are supplementary volumes which include many words still in use.

➤ Godefroy, Frédéric Eugène. Lexique de l'ancien français. Publié par les soins de Jean Bonnard et Amédée Salmon. Paris: Welter, 1901.

This is an abridged, one-volume version of Godefroy which omits many of the words and quotations which were included in the former title.

➤ Tobler, Adolf. Tobler-Lommatzsch, Altfranzösisches Wörterbuch; Adolf Toblers nachgelassene Materialien bearbeitet

43

und . . . herausgegeben von Erhard
Lommatzsch. . . . Berlin: Weidmann,
1925- . (In progress.)

This is an important scholarly dictionary
of the French language from the twelfth to
the fourteenth century, and is particularly
strong in the literary language. It includes
all words of those centuries whether still in
usage or not, and indicates parallels in other
Romance languages. Tobler-Lommatzsch gives
many examples of usage, history and etymology,
and references to published studies. While
many of the examples are given in ancien
français, definitions and all prefatory matter
are in German. The dictionary continues to
be published in Lieferungen (fascicles).

➤ Van Daele, Hilaire. Petit dictionnaire de
l'ancien français. Paris: Garnier, 1940.

This one-volume dictionary is good for
brief definitions of medieval French, but it
does not include quotations or extensive etymologies. It is most useful as a "reading"
dictionary, and is not designed for intensive
research into the language of the period.

Renaissance

➤ Grandsaignes d'Hauterive, Robert. Dictionnaire d'ancien français: Moyen âge
et renaissance. Paris: Larousse, 1947.

This one-volume dictionary of medieval and
Renaissance French includes words in use up
to the end of the sixteenth century with
examples of usage, etymology, spelling variants,
approximation of modern meaning, and the time

44

periods when these words were current. Words
are entered in their original spelling.

➤ Huguet, Edmond. Dictionnaire de la langue
    française du seizième siècle. Paris:
    Champion, Didier, 1925- . (In progress.)
    This scholarly multi-volume dictionary of
sixteenth century French is more comprehensive
than Grandsaignes d'Hauterive and includes
slang, words no longer in use, and those whose
meaning has changed. The quotations and
illustrative examples are given in the original
spelling, and there is a "Liste des ouvrages
auxquels sont empruntées les citations."
There is no pronunciation or etymology. The
dictionary is being published in fascicles.

Seventeenth Century

➤ Cayrou, Gaston. Le français classique:
    Lexique de la langue du dix-septième
    siècle. . . . 6. éd. Paris: Didier, 1948.
    This dictionary of classical French is
composed of 2,200 words taken from seventeenth
century dictionaries. It includes those words
whose meaning has changed and quotations from
major writers.

➤ Dubois, Jean; Lagane, René; and Leroud, Alain.
    Dictionnaire du français classique. Paris:
    Larousse, 1971.
    This dictionary includes more words (5,200)
and quotations from more authors than Cayrou.
While words are entered in modern spelling,
variations from the seventeenth century
spelling are noted. A list of authors and

abbreviations is appended at the front of the work.

Hatzfeld, Adolphe, and Darmesteter, Arsène. _Dictionnaire général de la langue française du commencement du XVIIe siècle jusqu'à nos jours_. 9. éd. Paris: Delagrave, 1932. (Reprinted 1964.)

This two-volume dictionary shows pronunciation, etymology, and the first use of words. While it may be somewhat more difficult to use than either Cayrou or Dubois because of the many abbreviations employed, it is particularly important to graduate students because of its 300 page discussion of the formation of the French language in volume one. The dictionary definitions are arranged in historical (i.e., chronological) order.

Huguet, Edmond. _Petit glossaire des classiques français du dix-septième siècle. . . ._ Paris: Hachette, 1907.

This dictionary is particularly well-suited to the needs of undergraduates. It contains clear definitions and documented quotations of those words and locutions "qui ont vieilli ou dont le sens s'est modifié." It does not contain as many words as Hatzfeld.

Livet, Charles Louis. _Lexique de la langue de Molière comparée à celle des écrivains de son temps, avec des commentaires de philologie historique et grammaticale. . . ._ Paris: Imprimerie nationale, 1895-97.

While this three-volume work is not technically a "dictionary," it is one of the most

46

important titles in lexicography of the seventeenth century, and will be particularly useful to graduate students. For each word there are illustrative quotations from Molière which are in turn followed by quotations from other prominent classical authors. Livet's Lexique was commended by the Académie française.

Nineteenth and Twentieth Centuries

➤ Dictionnaire du français contemporain. Par Jean Dubois [et al.]. Paris: Larousse, 1971.

While not really a "literary" dictionary, this title is important because it lists over 25,000 words, all of which are now a part of la langue parlée, and many of which will probably be incorporated into future editions of the "standard" dictionaries as they appear in the popular press and eventually in the literary language. The dictionary gives pronunciation, some synonyms and antonyms, and indicates correct usage. It is a useful adjunct to the standard unabridged and abridged dictionaries.

➤ Rheims, Maurice. Dictionnaire des mots sauvages (Ecrivains des XIXe et XXe siècles). Paris: Larousse, 1969.

This compilation of mots forgés and néologismes is excellent for the study of the language of modern literature, indicating usage and the literary context of each term. A good bibliography at the back of the volume gives full references to the words cited as well as a bibliography of dictionaries.

47

Etymological Dictionaries

The etymological dictionary seeks to establish the origin, formation, and development of words. While the standard and period dictionaries often include etymologies in their entries, the notations are necessarily brief, and so if you engaged in advanced language and linguistic studies, the following titles will be useful. For other titles, check in your library's catalog under the heading "French language--Etymology--Dictionaries."

➤ Bloch, Oscar, and Wartburg, Walther von. Dictionnaire étymologique de la langue française. 5. éd., revue et augmentée par W. von Wartburg. Paris: Presses Universitaires de France, 1968.

The preface to this work tells us that "L'objet d'un dictionnaire étymologique est d'expliquer le vocabulaire d'une langue," and this one-volume dictionary "à l'intention du public non spécialiste" fulfills its objective. A useful and reliable dictionary for both graduate and undergraduate students, it gives the earliest known dates of use (but no sources), full definitions, and many derivatives.

➤ Dauzat, Albert; Dubois, Jean; and Mitterand, Henri. Nouveau dictionnaire étymologique et historique. 2. éd. Paris: Larousse, 1971.

This work is contemporary in scope and popular in character and will be of most value to the undergraduate. Since it excludes some regional and archaic terms, it should be used

in conjunction with <u>Bloch</u> or the works listed
below (<u>Gamillscheg</u> or <u>Wartburg</u>).

➤ Gamillscheg, Ernst. <u>Etymologisches Wörterbuch</u>
<u>der französischen Sprache</u> . . . mit einem
Wort- und Sachverzeichnis von Heinrich
Kuen. 2. vollständig neu bearbeitet Auflage.
Heidelberg: Winter, 1966-69.
This German dictionary of French etymology
was originally published in 1928. It gives
German equivalents and the origins (with date--
usually century only) of words from all cen-
turies of the French language. It incorporates
Provincial French and also shows the roots of
words, including American, Arabic, and Greek.
<u>Gamillscheg</u> requires reading competence in
German and will be most useful to graduate
students.

➤ Wartburg, Walther von. <u>Französisches ety-</u>
<u>mologisches Wörterbuch; eine Darstellung</u>
<u>des galloromanischen Sprachschatzes</u>.
Bonn: Klopp; Basel: Helbing und Lichten-
halm, 1928- . (In progress. Reprinted:
Tübingen: J. C. B. Mohr, 1948- .)
This great German work is the most scholarly
and comprehensive of the French etymological
dictionaries and will be useful to advanced
graduate students who have reading competence
in German. Wartburg's dictionary has been
published serially since 1928 in <u>Lieferungen</u>
(fascicles), which were numbered consecutively
as issued, each forming part of different
volumes. The dictionary proper comprises
fourteen volumes; volumes fifteen through

seventeen (in various parts) cover "Germanische elemente" (German elements in French); volume eighteen "Anglizismen" (English elements); volume nineteen "Orientalia"; and volume twenty "Entlehnungen aus den übrigen Sprachen" (borrowed words from other languages). Beginning with volume twenty-one, the words from the main set are classified into subject categories (e.g., "L'univers"). Wartburg is complicated in arrangement, so you should plan to consult a reference librarian who may be able to help you make the most effective use of this great etymological dictionary.

Slang Dictionaries

The slang dictionary is a systematic listing of those words and expressions normally considered to be below the level of standard, educated speech because of their informality or their relationship to the "underworld" (frequently called "argot"). While the slang usage of standard vocabulary is documented in many of the unabridged and abridged dictionaries mentioned earlier, none will include the large number of slang expressions and colloquialisms to be found in the titles listed here. In this category there are two French slang dictionaries and two bilingual slang dictionaries. For other titles, check in your library's catalog under the heading "French language--Slang--Dictionaries."

➤ Esnault, Gaston. Dictionnaire historique des argots français. 2. éd. Paris: Larousse, 1966.

This is an important title since it frequently cites examples of early usage and often indicates etymology. When dates of usage are indicated with examples, you should consult the list of abbreviations which will indicate sources. Esnault is particularly useful as a retrospective work.

➤ Leitner, Moses Jonathon, and Lanen, J. R., eds. Dictionary of French and American Slang. New York: Crown, 1965.

This bilingual slang dictionary is divided into two sections: French-American and American-French, each preceded by a list of symbols and abbreviations. Entry is made under both words and phrases or expressions, and the dictionary is exceptionally easy to consult because of its clear typography and format. Many of the definitions are quite amusing: "bubble dancer: 'strip-teaseuse' qui utilise des ballons dans son numéro."

➤ Marks, Joseph. The New French-English Dictionary of Slang and Colloquialisms. Revised and completed by Georgette A. Marks and Albert J. Farmer. New York: E. P. Dutton, 1970.

This French-English work (there is no English-French section) is "not intended only for the specialist," and is decidedly British in orientation. It includes "very recent slang which may well turn out to be ephemeral" and a "Table of English Slang Synonyms." Phrases or expressions are normally entered under a "keyword," and so you would look for

the expression "être emballé pour (or sur)"
under the word "emballé."

➤ Sandry, Géo, and Carrère, Marcel. Dictionnaire de l'argot moderne. 9. éd.,
   revue et augmentée. Paris: Editions du
   Dauphin, 1967.
   While this slang compilation does not indicate etymology or dates of usage, it does
   include special vocabulary lists in subject
   categories such as business, racing, prison,
   etc.

Synonym Dictionaries

You have already seen that at least one unabridged dictionary (the Robert) includes synonyms,
but it is necessarily limited in the amount of
information it can supply. Compilations of synonyms
are designed to help you accurately discriminate
between similar words and will be particularly
useful when you are writing term papers and theses.
For other titles, check in your library's catalog
under the heading "French language--Synonyms and
antonyms."

➤ Bailly, René. Dictionnaire des synonymes de
   la langue française. Sous la direction de
   Michel de Toro. Paris: Larousse, 1972,
   (c1946).
   Bailly is a small, compact work which brings
   related words together and clearly and simply
   explains their differences, sometimes with
   examples. This dictionary was commended by
   the Académie française.

➤ Bénac, Henri. Dictionnaire des synonymes,

conforme au Dictionnaire de l'Académie
française. Paris: Hachette, 1956. (And
other reprintings.)

Bénac's synonym dictionary also gives
examples which illustrate differences in
meaning and also quotes many major French
authors with reference to sources. It is
slightly larger than Bailly.

Bilingual Dictionaries

The aim of the bilingual dictionary is to
accurately translate from one language to another.
As with the standard "all-French" dictionaries,
there are multi-volume unabridged and one-volume
abridged bilingual dictionaries. When your translation must be precise, you would be well advised
to turn to the larger, bilingual dictionary whose
explanations will obviously be more detailed. For
other bilingual dictionaries, check in your library's
catalog under the heading "French language--Dic-
tionaries--English."

➤ Deak, Etienne. Grand dictionnaire d'améri-
canismes, contenant les principaux termes
américains avec leur équivalent exact en
français. 4. éd. Paris: Editions du
Dauphin, 1966. (And other reprintings and
editions.)

This American-French dictionary is designed
for the French speaker who wants to translate
American slang and idiomatic expressions--it
includes such things as the names of various
cocktails. It will be a useful adjunct to
the "standard" bilingual dictionaries.

➤ Guiraud, Jules. <u>Dictionnaire anglais-français
à l'usage des professeurs, des littéra-
teurs</u>, [etc.]. 3. éd. Paris: Belin,
1947.

This two-volume dictionary (volume one,
English-French; volume two, French-English) is
rich in quotations from literary figures, but
also includes general and scientific terminology and proper names. Pronunciation is indicated and there are many examples showing
usage.

➤ <u>Harrap's Shorter French and English Dictionary
(French-English, English-French complete
in one volume)</u>. By J. E. Mansion. London, Toronto, etc.: Harrap, 1967. (And
other reprintings and editions.)

<u>Harrap's Shorter</u> (as it is commonly called)
is the abridged version of <u>Harrap's New Stan-
dard</u> (see below). It too includes pronunciation and examples of usage, and although there
is a British emphasis, American usage is indicated.

➤ <u>Harrap's New Standard French and English Dic-
tionary</u>. By J. E. Mansion. New York:
Charles Scribner's Sons, 1972.

<u>Harrap's</u> is larger and more current than
<u>Guiraud</u>. It is divided into two parts: part
one (French-English) is in two volumes; part
two (English-French) is in one volume. While
entry for English words is in British spelling
(e.g., "colour"), the dictionary does distinguish between British and American usage.
This highly detailed work is indispensable

since it now includes many new Americanisms.

➤ Larousse Modern French-English (English-French) Dictionary. By Marguerite-Marie Dubois [et al.]. New York: McGraw-Hill, 1960. (And other reprintings and editions.)

This illustrated one-volume Larousse dictionary includes slang and colloquial expressions but does not have as many examples of usage as does Harrap's Shorter. It does, however, indicate the meanings of a word within a special subject such as engineering.

➤ New Cassell's French Dictionary: French-English, English-French. Completely revised by Denis Girard [et al.]. New York: Funk and Wagnalls, 1973. (And other reprintings and editions.)

Cassell's is a standard one-volume desk dictionary that defines both words and expressions. Spelling is in American English and pronunciation is indicated. Cassell's also includes some useful appendices such as weights and measures and French and English abbreviations.

Subject Dictionaries

This type of dictionary, sometimes called a "glossary," defines terms used in a special subject field--in our case, literature. While there are many titles available, the following words are representative of what you should expect to find in a good subject dictionary. For other subject dictionaries, check in your library's catalog under the following subject headings: "French litera-

55

ture--Dictionaries," "Literature--Dictionaries,"
and "Literature--Terminology."

➤ Beckson, Karl E., and Ganz, Arthur F.
Literary Terms: A Dictionary. New York:
Farrar, Straus and Giroux, 1975.
This is a revised and updated version of
the authors' work which was originally published in 1961. It includes definitions of
many recent critical terms such as "New novel."

➤ Fowler, Roger. Dictionary of Modern Critical
Terms. London, Boston: Routledge and
Kegan Paul, 1973.
This is a useful adjunct to the short-entry
dictionary, for it contains larger discursive
entries on many of the most frequently used
terms. Its aim is to "add to and qualify
such aids [as Shipley, etc.] by encouraging
a new perspective on literary terminology."

➤ Redfern, James. A Glossary of French Literary
Expression. See entry in the category
"Books on Usage and Grammars."

➤ Shaw, Harry. Dictionary of Literary Terms.
New York: McGraw-Hill, 1972.
Shaw defines over 2,000 critical terms used
in literature, and in other related fields such
as journalism, television, film, and stage.

➤ Shipley, Joseph Twadell, ed. Dictionary of
World Literary Terms: Forms, Technique,
Criticism. 3rd ed., completely revised and
enlarged. Boston: The Writer, Inc., 1970.
Shipley's work is divided into three parts:
a dictionary of terms, forms, definitions,

techniques, types and genres; critical surveys of most national literatures (including
French); and a selected list of critics from
other countries.

Books on Usage and Grammars

While works on usage and grammar are not
technically "dictionaries," they do form an important part of the "word-book" category. Since dictionaries cannot possibly address the problems of
syntax, grammar, and usage in a comprehensive way,
you should turn to any of the following titles
which will help you to develop competence and confidence when speaking and writing French. For
other similar works, check in your library's
catalog under "French language--Grammar--1950-   ,"
and "French language--Usage."

➤   Bescherelle, Louis Nicolas. L'art de con-
        juguer, dictionnaire des huit mille verbes
        usuels. Paris: Hatier, 1969. (And other
        reprintings.)
        Bescherelle contains a discussion of the
grammatical peculiarities of French verbs, over
eighty tables conjugating verb "types," and
an index of the "huit mille verbes usuels."
The index refers you to the "type" verb (and
not to page number) which is conjugated in the
various moods and tenses.

➤   Colin, Jean Paul. Nouveau dictionnaire des
        difficultés du français. Paris: Hachette-
        Tchon, 1971.
        This small, one-volume work is an alpha-
betically arranged list of those words which

traditionally pose difficult orthographic or usage problems. Among other things, it will help you to distinguish between words of nearly the same spelling and tell you whether or not a word is hyphenated.

➤ Dupré, Paul. <u>Encyclopédie du bon français dans l'usage contemporain</u>. Paris: Editions de Trévise, 1972.

This is an excellent three-volume dictionary of "difficultés, subtilités, complexités [et] singularités." Arranged alphabetically, the <u>Encyclopédie</u> shows what the standard French dictionaries have to say about the usage of a word by bringing together the opinions of eminent lexicographers and indicating what consensus, if any, exists. Dupré's work is an indispensable tool for any student of French.

➤ <u>Grammaire Larousse du français contemporain</u>. [Par] Jean-Claude Chevalier [<u>et al</u>.]. Paris: Larousse, 1971. (And other re-printings and editions.)

This Larousse grammar is divided into the following parts: "les éléments constituants du discours," "les parties du discours," and "la versification." It contains a detailed index and concise statements on usage.

➤ Grevisse, Maurice. <u>Le bon usage</u>. 9. éd. Gembloux: Editions J. Duculot; Paris: Hatier, 1969. (And other reprintings and editions.)

This standard work is divided into the following parts: "éléments de la langue," "la proposition," "les parties du discours,"

and "les propositions subordonées," each of
which is subdivided into several chapters.
An extensive bibliography of works on grammar
and language is included at the front of the
work. Grevisse's Le bon usage is the source
for detailed and definitive information on
usage and grammar.

▶ Grevisse, Maurice. Précis de grammaire
française. Gembloux: Editions J. Duculot,
1969. (And other reprintings and editions.)
Grevisse's Précis is a shortened and more
easily usable version of his Le bon usage,
containing much of the same information but
presented in a less technical fashion. It is
divided into various parts and subdivided by
sections.

▶ Hennebert, Jean. Au lieu de, dites plutôt.
Paris: Mercure de France, 1968.
The subtitle of this book indicates its
scope: "Le bon usage en exemples pratiques."
Hennebert emphasizes the spoken and journalis-
tic language and discusses many of the common
errors in differentiating one word from
another. The index is inside the front cover.

▶ Lasserre, Emilie. Est-ce à ou de? 11. éd.
Lausanne: Payot, 1969. (And other reprintings.)
This pamphlet-like work is an indispensable
"répertoire des verbes, adjectifs et locutions
se construisant avec une préposition." It
is divided into three parts: an alphabetically
arranged list of verbs and adjectives showing
usage with (or without) prepositions, a section

59

on "locutions à valeur verbale," and a section
on "locutions à valeur prépositive."

► Redfern, James. _A Glossary of French Literary
Expression_. New York: Harcourt, 1970.
This title is similar in some ways to the
special "subject" dictionaries discussed earlier, for it includes many critical terms. Its
purpose is to help the student write better
compositions, and it lists, in alphabetical
order, "virtually all the entries listed in
the _Vocabulaire d'initiation à la critique et
à l'explication littéraire_ published in Paris
by the Ministère de l'éducation nationale."
Entry is made under the _English_ word and then
either defined or illustrated in a clause or
sentence (usually the latter). It includes
regular words (e.g., "feel" and "flavor") and
literary terminology (e.g., "octosyllable" and
"onomatopœia").

ENCYCLOPEDIAS

Encyclopedias are useful information sources
for answering general questions on persons, places,
or things. While you are undoubtedly familiar with
such general-purpose English language encyclopedias
as the _Britannica_ and _Americana_--or in the French
language, the various Larousse titles, the _Encyc-
lopedia Universalis_, and _La Grande encyclopédie_--you
may not have been aware of the existence of what
librarians often call "special subject" encyclopedias. These works will give you concise but
useful overviews of authors, characters, works, and
movements. Some of the titles in this category deal

60

only with French literature, while others broaden
their scope to include the other national literatures. For other general purpose and special subject encyclopedias, check in your library's catalog
under the headings "Encyclopedias and dictionaries,
French," "France--Dictionaries and encyclopedias,"
"French literature--Dictionaries," and "Literature--
Dictionaries."

➤ Braun, Sidney David, ed. Dictionary of French
Literature. New York: Philosophical
Library, 1958.

This illustrated "dictionary" covers all
periods of literary activity and includes biographies (some with bibliographies), short
summaries of important works, surveys of
literary genres and movements, definitions of
literary terms, and some articles on the
French language. It is similar in scope to
the Oxford Companion discussed in this section.

➤ Cassell's Encyclopedia of World Literature.
Revised and enlarged edition edited by J.
Buchanan-Brown. New York: W. Morrow, 1973.

Originally published in 1953 as Cassell's
Encyclopedia of Literature, this newly-revised
three-volume set is arranged as follows:
volume one, histories and general articles on
genres, literary forms, etc.; volume two, biographies, A-K; volume three, biographies, L-Z.
The articles are signed and frequently include
bibliographies.

➤ The Concise Oxford Dictionary of French Literature. Edited by Joyce M. H. Reid. New
York: Oxford University Press, 1976.

61

This is an abridged and revised version of
the Oxford Companion effected by "condensation
and amalgamation rather than omission." New
articles have been added and existing articles
have been revised and expanded.

➤ Dictionnaire des lettres françaises. Publié
   sous la direction du Cardinal Georges
   Grente. Paris: Arthème Fayard, 1951-73.

This multi-volume encyclopedia includes articles on persons, academies, universities, and
literary subjects, with each volume covering a
particular period. Articles are signed and contain bibliographies of the works of authors as
well as critical materials about both authors
and subjects.

➤ Dictionnaire des œuvres de tous les temps et
   de tous les pays: Littérature, philosophie,
   musique, sciences. [Par] Laffont-Bompiani.
   3. éd. Paris: Société d'éditions de dic-
   tionnaires et encyclopédies [S.E.D.E.], 1958.
---Supplément 1959. Paris: S.E.D.E., 1959.
Dictionnaire des œuvres contemporaines de tous
   les pays. . . . Paris: S.E.D.E., 1967.

Laffont-Bompiani (named after its editors,
Robert Laffont and Valentino Bompiani) is composed of the basic four-volume set, a "Supplément" of addenda and an index to authors, and
the Dictionnaire des œuvres contemporaines
which forms the fifth and final volume. This
latter volume contains entries for works by
authors who died after 1955 or who were born
after 1910. Copiously illustrated, Laffont-
Bompiani enters under the translated French

title of works followed by the original title in brackets. Articles are not signed.[2]

➤ Dictionnaire des personnages littéraires et
   dramatiques de tous les temps et de tous les
   pays: Poésie, théâtre, roman, musique. [Par]
   Laffont-Bompiani. Paris: S.E.D.E., 1960.

   This volume, also edited by Laffont and Bompiani, complements the previous set, and consists of articles on literary characters and
   their significance in literature, with cross-
   references to the Dictionnaire des œuvres de
   tous les temps et de tous les pays.

➤ Dictionnaire universel des lettres. Publié
   sous la direction de Pierre Clarac. Paris:
   S.E.D.E., 1961.

   This one-volume "ready-reference" encyclopedia is an abridgment of the Laffont-Bompiani works cited above, and would be suitable
   for home use.

➤ Harvey, Sir Paul, and Heseltine, Janet E.
   The Oxford Companion to French Literature.
   Oxford: Clarendon Press, 1959.

   The Oxford Companion is an excellent one-
   volume handbook of authors, titles, critics,
   places, allusions, literary terms, and forms
   (e.g., "Dictionaries and encyclopedias").
   While there are no bibliographies, there are
   often lists of an author's most important works
   following the entry. You might consider the
   purchase of this title.

➤ Pingaud, Bernard. Ecrivains d'aujourd'hui,
   1940-1960: Dictionnaire anthologique et

critique. Paris: Grasset, 1960.

Although primarily a biographical source, Pingaud includes extracts of the authors' writings as well as some critical evaluations. Besides the signed articles on forty-nine authors, there is also a critical essay by Robert Kanten entitled "Point de vue" at the back of the volume. Most of the articles include bibliographies of works by and about the authors.

BIOGRAPHICAL SOURCES

Biographical information can be found in the general French encyclopedias, the encyclopedias of literature, and in the general biographical dictionaries such as the Dictionnaire de biographie française, Michaud's Biographie universelle, or the Nouveau dictionnaire national des contemporains. There are also, however, some special biographical sources which deal exclusively with authors. In general, these sources will give you useful information on the lives and literary contributions of writers with bibliographies of works by and about them. For both general and special biographical sources, check in your library's catalog under the headings "France--Biography," "France--Bio-bibliography," "Authors, French--Biography," "Authors, French--Bio-bibliography," "French literature--Bio-bibliography," "French literature--History and criticism," and, of course, under the names of individual authors. You might also find some important titles under the more general headings "Bio-bibliography--Dictionaries," "Biography--

Dictionaries," and "Literature--Bio-bibliography."

➤ Boisdeffre, Pierre de, ed. Dictionnaire de
    littérature contemporaine. Par R. M. Al-
    bérès, [et al.]. Nouvelle éd. mise à jour.
    Paris: Editions Universitaires, 1963.
    This illustrated work includes signed
articles on twentieth century French writers,
bibliographies of the authors' works, and
references to other biographical material.
Nine introductory essays survey French literature of the twentieth century.

➤ Dictionnaire biographique des auteurs de tous
    les temps et de tous les pays. [Par]
    Laffont-Bompiani. 2. éd. Paris: S.E.D.E.,
    1964.
    This two-volume biographical dictionary
(volume one, A-J; volume two, K-Z) is profusely
illustrated and complements the Dictionnaire
des œuvres (discussed in the previous section) to which there are cross-references.
The unsigned articles critically evaluate an
author's contributions to literature and include bibliographies. The work is universal
in scope.

➤ Havlice, Patricia P. Index to Literary Bio-
    graphy. Metuchen, N.J.: Scarecrow, 1975.
    This work indexes fifty common and uncommon
sources for biographical material on American
and continental authors.

➤ Kunitz, Stanley Jasspon, and Colby, Vineta,
    eds. European Authors, 1000-1900: A
    Biographical Dictionary of European Litera-

ture. New York: H. W. Wilson, 1967.

This biographical source contains biographies of 967 continental writers (those who
were born after 1000 or who died before 1925),
and includes 309 portraits. The signed articles contain bibliographies of works by and
about the writers.

➤ Malignon, Jean. Dictionnaire des écrivains
   français. Paris: Editions du Seuil, 1971.

Malignon's work contains articles under
headings for individual authors and for "types"
of authors such as "Chroniqueurs du Moyen
âge." A well-designed book with many excellent illustrations and portraits, the articles include bibliographies of works by and
about French writers. There is also a "Tableau
chronologique" of historical, literary, and
cultural events at the back of the volume.

➤ Pingaud, Bernard. Ecrivains d'aujourd'hui,
   1940-1960. . . . See entry in the category
   "Encyclopedias."

➤ Wakeman, John, and Kunitz, Stanley J. World
   Authors, 1950-1970: A Companion Volume to
   "Twentieth Century Authors". New York:
   H. W. Wilson, 1975.

This biographical dictionary is useful for
access to information on newer authors who
reached prominence between 1950 and 1970. Included are world authors of science fiction,
gothic novels, and other popular forms of
literature.

Both the encyclopedia and biographical sources provide answers to specific questions. Histories go one step further by providing specific information as well as a general context. While there are literally hundreds of histories available, the following titles are certainly representative. For other histories, check in your library's catalog under the heading "French literature" with the following subdivisions: "--To 1500," "--16th century," "--17th century," "--18th century," "--19th century," and "--20th century." You may also find information under the headings "Pléiades" (for the sixteenth century) and "Précieuses" (for the seventeenth century).

➤ Adam, Antoine; Lerminier, Georges; and Morot-Sir, Edouard. <u>Littérature française</u>. Paris: Larousse, 1967-68.

This two-volume set serves to update the standard "Bédier/Hazard" history (see page 69). Each volume contains a bibliography, index, and detailed table of contents. Volume two features several short articles on literature of French expression outside of France. Both volumes are profusely illustrated.

➤ Brereton, Geoffrey. <u>A Short History of French Literature</u>. 2nd ed. Baltimore: Penguin, 1976.

This 368 page paperback history of French literature would be most useful as a "ready-reference" tool for your home personal library. It includes a bibliography and index.

➤ Calvet, Jean. <u>Histoire de la littérature
   française</u>. Paris: De Gigord, 1955-64.
   This ten-volume illustrated history is
written from a Catholic point of view. Each
volume is devoted to a different period of
literature and there are good bibliographies
and indexes in each volume.

➤ Godefroy, Frédéric Eugène. <u>Histoire de la
   littérature française depuis le XVIe siècle
   jusqu'à nos jours</u>. 2. éd. Paris: Gaume,
   1878-81.
   This history, "couronné par l'Académie française," is particularly useful for its nineteenth century viewpoint. While there is no index, there is a fairly detailed "Table de matières" at the back of each of the ten volumes.

➤ <u>Histoire littéraire de la France</u>. Ouvrage
   commencé par les religieux bénédictins de la
   Congrégation de Saint Maur, et continué par
   des membres de l'Institut (Académie des inscriptions et belles-lettres). Paris: Imprimerie nationale, 1733- . (In progress.)
   This is the most detailed of all French histories: the latest volume to appear (volume
thirty-nine, 1962) is only partly through the
fourteenth century. The history consists most-
ly of critical articles on authors, and later
volumes are particularly important for their
copious bibliographical references. This work
would very probably be useful only to the advanced graduate student specializing in medieval literature.

➤ Lanson, Gustave. <u>Histoire de la littérature</u>

française. Remaniée et complétée pour la
période 1850-1950 par Paul Tuffrau. Paris:
Hachette, 1952.

This is an important "standard" one-volume
work that you might consider for purchase.

➤ Littérature française. [Par] Joseph Bédier [et]
Paul Hazard. Nouvelle éd., sous la direction de Pierre Martino. Paris: Larousse,
1948-49.

This reputable (but dated) history in two
volumes covers the history of French literature
up to the 1940s. It is lavishly illustrated.

➤ Manuel d'histoire littéraire de la France. Par
un collectif sous la direction de Pierre
Abraham et de Roland Desné. Paris: Editions Sociales, 1965- . (In progress.)

This multi-volume history is notable for
indicating relationships between literary and
linguistic, social, economic, and political
movements. Although there is no index, there
are important bibliographies as well as
"tableaux chronologiques."

➤ Petit de Julleville, Louis. Histoire de la
langue et de la littérature française des
origines à 1900. Paris: Colin, 1896-99.

While obviously dated, this illustrated
eight-volume history is still useful for its
bibliographies.

➤ Pichois, Claude. Littérature française: Collection. Paris: Arthaud, 1968- . (In progress.)

This illustrated history, when completed,
will number sixteen volumes. Comprehensive and

up-to-date in its critical evaluations of both
French literary and artistic evolution, it also
includes "tables chronologiques" and bio-bib-
liographical information.

➤ Queneau, Raymond, ed. Littératures françaises,
    connexes et marginales. Volume three of
    Histoire des littératures. Paris: Galli-
    mard, 1958. (Reprinted 1972.)
    This third volume in the "Bibliothèque de la
Pléiade" series, Histoire des littératures, is
particularly important for its treatment of
literature of French expression outside of
France and its discussion of modern popular
literature such as science fiction.

BIBLIOGRAPHIC GUIDES

Bibliographic guides indicate the most important sources and materials in a subject field. While
we will deal here with the guides to French literature, you should also be aware of the following general guides to reference works, each of which lists
bibliographies, encyclopedias, almanacs, etc., in
almost every field of study. For other similar
guides, check in your library's catalog under the
heading "Reference books--Bibliography."

➤ Malclès, Louise-Noëlle. Manuel de biblio-
    graphie. 2. éd. Paris: Presses Univer-
    sitaires de France, 1969.

➤ Malclès, Louise-Noëlle. Les Sources du travail
    bibliographique. Genève: Droz, 1950-58.

➤ Sheehy, Eugene P. Guide to Reference Books.
    9th ed. Chicago: American Library Associa-

tion, 1976. (This latest edition supersedes Constance M. Winchell's eighth edition and its supplements.)

The bibliographic guides to French literature are indispensable tools that will help you to identify the most authoritative editions of an author's works as well as the best critical studies. Some concentrate on listing bibliographies which have been devoted to special subjects or individual authors. Almost any of the guides listed below will save you a great deal of time and should always be consulted immediately when you begin to conduct research for a term paper or thesis. For other titles, check in your library's catalog under the headings "Reference books--French literature--Bibliography," "Bibliography--Bibliography--French literature," and "Bibliography--Bibliography--France."

➤ Bassan, Fernande, [et al.]. An Annotated Bibliography of French Language and Literature. New York: Garland, 1976.

This compilation is addressed to the "English-speaking reader with some knowledge of French," and is divided into the following parts: general bibliographies and reference works, general studies on the French language, and bibliographical studies of literature.

➤ Bouvier, Emile, and Jourda, Pierre. Guide de l'étudiant en littérature française. 6. éd. Paris: Presses Universitaires de France, 1968.

While written for the French university student, this guide is helpful as a general orientation to the French scholarly method and

includes material on "les méthodes d'exposi-
tion" and "les méthodes de l'histoire littéraire" as well as "les instruments de travail
de l'histoire littéraire."

➤ Cordié, Carlo. Avviamento allo studio della
  lingua e della letteratura francese.
  Milan: Carlo Marzorati, 1955.

  This bibliographic guide is divided into
three parts: a listing of general reference
works, a listing of works devoted to French
literature (arranged chronologically by
period), and a long bibliographic essay on
French literary history. Only works published
up to 1954 are included. Reading competence
in Italian is essential.

➤ Kirsop, Wallace. "The Bibliography of French
  Literary History: Progress, Problems,
  Projects." Australian Journal of French
  Studies 1 (1964): 325-364.

  Kirsop's discursive article is not technically a bibliographic guide, but it does include information on some little-used sources.
Designed as a "state-of-the-art" survey for
advanced researchers, it will be most useful
to advanced graduate students who have a sound
working knowledge of the bibliographic apparatus of the field.

➤ Langlois, Pierre, and Mareuil, André. Guide
  bibliographique des études littéraires.
  3. éd. Paris: Hachette, 1965.

  This guide was prepared for the professor
of French literature who found himself in one
of the small provincial French colleges whose

72

library did not have all of the necessary tools for literary study. The bulk of the work is composed of a selective listing of the most important editions of French authors and important critical studies. It also includes a section on classical literature and an appendix which lists the most important studies of genres and literary history by foreign critics. You might consider the purchase of this title.

➤ Mahaffey, Denis. Concise Bibliography of
    French Literature. New York: Bowker, 1975.

Mahaffey's work ". . . attempts to supply basic bibliographical information on the outstanding features of French literature and scholarship, with details of English translations." The Concise Bibliography is arranged by century and includes "titles of critical works, biographies and lives."

➤ Osburn, Charles B. Research and Reference
    Guide to French Studies. Metuchen, N.J.:
    Scarecrow Press, 1968.

---Guide to French Studies: Supplement with
    Cumulative Indexes. Metuchen, N.J.:
    Scarecrow Press, 1972.

This greatly detailed bibliographic guide lists bibliographies not only for general French studies but also for individual authors. It also includes sections on "Comparative literature and travel," "Romance philology," etc. There are author and subject indexes in both volumes and analytical tables of contents. This is an indispensable tool for both graduates and undergraduates.

73

➤ Osburn, Charles B., ed. The Present State
of French Studies: A Collection of Research
Reviews. Metuchen, N.J.: Scarecrow Press,
1971.

This one-volume "state-of-the-art" survey
contains essays on "research and interpreta-
tion in more than forty topics of French literature from the middle ages through the
twentieth century," each written by a scholar
in the field. There are two important appendices: supplementary bibliographical essays
and a bibliography of additional research
reviews. It is a useful complement to any of
the guides listed in this section.

➤ Varillon, François, and Holstein, Henri.
Bibliographie élémentaire de littérature
française: Choix méthodique d'éditions
et d'études critiques. Paris: De Gigord,
1936.

While dated, this annotated bibliographic
guide indicates the best editions of French
literature from the middle ages to the nineteenth century. Important critical works
follow the list of "textes" of each author.
This is only one of the many earlier bibliographic guides which might serve you well
in a retrospective search for materials on a
subject.

BIBLIOGRAPHIES OF BIBLIOGRAPHIES

Bibliographies of bibliographies are useful
information sources that list bibliographies which
have been published as separate works, at the end

of books or periodical articles, or in collections
(such as Festschriften). Although you will not be
able to retrieve all pertinent bibliographies by
using these tools--all of them have certain re-
quirements as to the length of the bibliography
before it can be included--you can save time and
energy by using the bibliography of bibliographies
in tandem with the bibliographic guides mentioned
above. The subject heading in your library's
catalog for these tools is "Bibliography--Biblio-
graphy."

➤ Arnim, Max. Internationale Personalbiblio-
graphie, 1800-1943. Leipzig: Hiersemann,
1944-52.
---Band III, 1944-1959 und Nachträge, von
Gerhard Bock und Franz Hodes. Stuttgart:
Hiersemann, 1961-63.
This important three-volume work lists
bibliographies about persons that have appeared
in books, periodicals, annuals, biographical
dictionaries, etc., and is a good source for
both biographical and bibliographical citations.

➤ Besterman, Theodore. A World Bibliography of
Bibliographies and of Bibliographical Cata-
logues, Calendars, Abstracts, Digests,
Indexes, and the like. 4th ed. Lausanne:
Societas Bibliographica, 1965-66.
Besterman's monumental five-volume work
is a standard reference tool that contains
117,000 separate entries under both persons
and subjects. Although dated (it includes
bibliographies published through 1963), it can

be useful as a starting point for retrospective study. The arrangement of bibliographies under an author's name is chronological.

➤ Bibliographic Index: A Cumulative Bibliography of Bibliographies. New York: Wilson, 1938- .

This serial publication began coverage of English language books and periodicals in 1937 with entries under both subjects and personal names. While general in subject scope, you will often find entries under many of the major French authors.

BIBLIOGRAPHIES

For centuries, humanity has dreamed of being able to list every piece of recorded information in one place. Neither librarians nor scholars still believe that such a "master bibliography" is possible, although several attempts have been made. The most that any of us can realistically hope for is a "relatively comprehensive" bibliography by using the information sources listed in this section.

Library Catalogs

Did you ever consider a library catalog to be a "bibliography?" Indeed, the printed catalogs of the great national libraries (and only three are included here) are perhaps the closest we may ever come to "comprehensive" bibliography. Why? Because almost all of the national libraries serve as a copyright depository for books published within (and sometimes outside of) their borders. (In

France, the first law of dépôt légal was passed in 1537.) Furthermore, each national library also collects materials published almost anywhere in the world. While no single library catalog can hope to approach "universality," using all of them together can give you relative comprehensiveness.[3] For other catalogs, look in your library's catalog under the name of the individual library.

France

➤ Paris. Bibliothèque nationale. Catalogue général des livres imprimés: Auteurs. Paris: Imprimerie nationale, 1897- . (In progress.)

The "author" catalog of the great BN has been in progress since 1897 and is still not yet complete. When using it, you must remember that each volume will include only those titles which had been acquired by the library up to the date of publication of that volume, and in any case only up to 1959. From 1960, coverage is continued by the following title.

➤ Paris. Bibliothèque nationale. Catalogue général des livres imprimés: Auteurs-- collectivités-auteurs--anonymes, 1960-1964. Paris: Imprimerie nationale, 1965- . (In progress.)

This catalog picks up where the previous Catalogue général will leave off, in 1959. It includes corporate entries, anonymous publications, and authors for the period 1960-1964.

United States

➤ U.S. Library of Congress. A Catalog of Books

Represented by Library of Congress Printed Cards, Issued to July 31, 1942. Ann Arbor: Edwards, 1942-46.

This is just one of several different series of catalogs of the collections of the Library of Congress, our "national" library. Besides this particular 167 volume set, there are also subject catalogs which cover various periods of acquisition. The Library of Congress catalogs (and the National Union Catalog which is discussed below) are indispensable sources of bibliographic information because of the high quality of cataloging.

➤ National Union Catalog: Pre-1956 Imprints. A cumulative author list representing Library of Congress printed cards and titles reported by other American libraries. London: Mansell, 1968- , v.1- .

As its title indicates, this "union catalog" lists pre-1956 imprints that are held both in the Library of Congress and in many of the largest North American libraries. When complete, this NUC will be in some 600 volumes, with approximately 10,000,000 entries, and will supersede the Library of Congress catalogs and supplements that covered acquisitions up to that period.

➤ National Union Catalog: A Cumulative Author List. Washington: Library of Congress Card Division, 1956- .

This is a monthly publication with quarterly and annual cumulations which continues the coverage provided by the "Pre-1956 Imprints"

78

NUC. As with the former title, this serially
published catalog includes both Library of
Congress holdings as well as the holdings of
major American and some Canadian libraries.

Great Britain

► British Museum. Department of Printed Books.
General Catalogue of Printed Books. London:
Trustees of the British Museum, 1965-66.
The General Catalogue of the British Museum
is a 263-volume set that is supplemented by
various serial publications including an annual
Additions and a Subject Index.

► British Museum. Department of Printed Books.
Short-Title Catalogue of Books Printed in
France and of French Books Printed in Other
Countries from 1470 to 1600 now in the
British Museum. London: Trustees of the
British Museum, 1924.
A useful complement to the catalog of the
Bibliothèque nationale, this catalog lists some
12,000 editions with the usual bibliographic
information.

► British Museum. Department of Printed Books.
A Short-Title Catalogue of French Books,
1601-1700, in the Library of the British
Museum. By V. F. Goldsmith. Folkestone:
Dawsons of Pall Mall, 1969- , fasc. 1- .
Similar in scope to the previous Short-Title
Catalogue . . . 1470-1600, this catalog will
contain some 35,000 entries including some
accessions not listed in the General Catalogue,
and three collections of "mazarinades" (works
on Cardinal Mazarin).

79

"Universal" Bibliographies

The term "universal" is often applied to the
two bibliographies listed below because they were
attempts to list general, rare, important, or note-
worthy books from any period or in any language.
While they are not by any means really "universal,"
they are considered to be standard reference sources
for information on early and rare books. Both
titles listed here are particularly important to
the bibliophile who may be interested in auction
prices, provenance, and other bibliographic and
critical notes. For other titles, check in your
library's catalog under the heading "Bibliography--
Early printed books."

➤ Brunet, Jacques Charles. _Manuel du libraire et_
de l'amateur de livres. 5. éd. Paris:
Didot, 1860-80.

While "universal" in scope, Brunet's _Manuel_
is particularly strong for French titles. The
main set is in five volumes, with four added
volumes containing subject indexes and supplements.

➤ Grässe, Johann Georg Theodor. _Trésor de livres_
rares et précieux. Dresden: Kuntze,
1859-69.

This seven-volume set is stronger in German
titles than Brunet's _Manuel_, but also contains
some titles not found in the Brunet set. Both
works should be used together in order to
achieve any comprehensiveness.

National and Trade Bibliographies

When librarians speak of "national and trade"

bibliographies, they are referring to those bibliographies which systematically list the publication
output of a particular country during a particular
period. These bibliographies are "enumerative" in
character and are often compiled from the records
supplied by individual trade publishers, although
such publications as dissertations and theses are
sometimes included. You will turn to the national
and trade bibliographies when you want to compile
special bibliographies, to verify bibliographical
citations, or perhaps even to verify the price of
a particular work.

The titles in this section are arranged in
chronological order by period of coverage, and you
will immediately note that coverage begins in the
eighteenth century. For books published prior to
1700, you can turn to library catalogs and to
descriptive bibliographies (e.g., the Répertoire
bibliographique des livres imprimés en France au
seizième siècle [Baden-Baden: Heitz, 1968- ,
Fasc. 1-] or Avenir Tchemerzine's Bibliographie
d'éditions originales et rares d'auteurs français
des XVe, XVIe, XVIIe et XVIIIe siècles. . . .
[Paris: M. Plée, 1927-34. 10 vol.]).

Since the scope of this book precludes an extensive discussion of the history and complexities
of the French national and trade bibliographies,
you may wish to turn to Louise-Noëlle Malclès's
Les Sources du travail bibliographique (volume one,
p. 138), where a chronological table of French
national bibliographies is presented. A competent
reference librarian may also be of assistance.

For other French national and trade bibliographies, you may also check in your library's

81

catalog under the subject heading "France--Imprints."

➤ Quérard, Joseph Marie. La France littéraire,
　ou dictionnaire bibliographique des savants,
　historiens et gens de lettres de la France,
　ainsi que des littérateurs étrangers qui
　ont écrit en français, plus particulièrement
　pendant les XVIIIe et XIXe siècles. Paris:
　Didot, 1827-64.
　This twelve-volume set is arranged alpha-
　betically by author. Volumes eleven and
　twelve are supplements.

➤ Quérard, Joseph Marie, [et al.]. La littéra-
　ture française contemporaine, 1827-1849.
　Dictionnaire bibliographique . . . accom-
　pagné de biographies et de notes historiques
　et littéraires. Paris: Daguin, 1842-57.
　This six-volume set continues the author's
　La France littéraire with the same alphabetical
　arrangement.

➤ Catalogue général de la librairie française,
　1840-1925. Paris: Lorenz, 1867-1945.
　This useful bibliography of nineteenth and
　twentieth century imprints is frequently cited
　as "Lorenz" and is composed of thirty-four
　volumes, each arranged alphabetically for the
　covered (from three to twenty-five years).
　There are also brief biographical notes on the
　authors and broad subject headings.

➤ Bibliographie de la France--Biblio. Paris:
　Cercle de la librairie, 1811-　, v.1-　.
　This is the "official" weekly list of French
　books which was Bibliographie de la France
　until 1971. Since 1972, it has cumulated

annually into <u>Les Livres de l'année--Biblio</u>
which is the merger of <u>Biblio</u> (discussed below)
and the <u>Bibliographie de la France</u>. The weekly
<u>Bibliographie de la France</u> (or <u>BF</u>) is arranged
in three parts, the most important of which is
called "Annonces" and contains <u>Les Livres de
la semaine</u> (which cumulates in <u>Les Livres du
mois</u>, then into <u>Les Livres du trimestre</u>, and
finally into <u>Les Livres du semestre</u>.

➤ <u>Biblio. Catalogue des ouvrages parus en langue
française dans le monde entier</u>. Paris:
Service bibliographique des messageries
Hachette, 1935- , v.1- .
Prior to its merger with the <u>Bibliographie
de la France</u>, this was a monthly publication
which cumulated annually. As its subtitle
indicates, <u>Biblio</u> includes French language
books published throughout the world. Since
1972, the annual cumulation has been super-
seded by <u>Les Livres de l'année--Biblio</u>.

➤ <u>Les Livres de l'année--Biblio</u>. Paris: Cercle
de la librairie, 1972- .
This annual cumulation of what were formerly
<u>Bibliographie de la France</u> and <u>Biblio</u> began
coverage of 1971 imprints in 1972.

➤ <u>Catalogue de l'édition française</u>. 1-   éd.;
1971- . Port Washington, N.Y.: Paris
Publications, 1971- .
This is the French equivalent of our <u>Books
in Print</u>, telling you what works on a publisher's list are still available for purchase.
The third edition of the <u>Catalogue</u>, published
in 1974, was in six volumes with the following

83

arrangement: volume one (in two parts),
"Auteurs"; volume two (in two parts), "Titres";
and volume three (in two parts), "Sujets."

Bibliographies of Anonyma and Pseudonyma

Did Voltaire or Pascal ever write under pseudonyms, initialisms, or anagrams? The bibliographies of anonyma and pseudonyma can answer such
questions. As an undergraduate, you will not often
need such tools, but whether you are an undergraduate or a graduate, you must be aware that the
standard French bibliographies will not indicate
anonymous works, nor will they attribute authorship.
If you are doing research into a period of some
political or religious turmoil, it is quite possible that some writings will have been published
under "des anagrammes, des astéronymes, des crypto-
nymes," etc.

For other such bibliographies, look in your
library's catalog under the following subject headings: "Anonyms and pseudonyms--Bibliography" and
"Anonyms and pseudonyms, French--Bibliography."

➤ Brunet, Gustave. Dictionnaire des ouvrages
anonymes, suivi des Supercheries littéraires dévoilées. . . . Paris: Féchoz,
1889.

This work is a supplement to Quérard's
Supercheries and to Barbier's Dictionnaire
(see below).

➤ Quérard, Joseph Marie. Les Supercheries
littéraires dévoilées. . . . 2. éd.
Paris: Daffis, 1869-70.

This second edition of Quérard's work

(volumes one through three, 1869-70) also includes Antoine-Alexandre Barbier's <u>Dictionnaire
des ouvrages anonymes</u> (volumes four through
seven, 1872-79).

Bibliographies of Literature and Criticism

The bibliographies of French literature and
criticism are the key tools for any research you
are conducting since they will list new editions of
an author's works as well as works about that
author (books, articles, dissertations, etc.). The
format of the bibliographies listed below is quite
uniform, being composed of a preface or introduction (which explains the scope of the work), a
table of contents (in the back of those works published in France), a list of abbreviations (usually
periodical titles), the bibliography, and any
indexes (author and subject). Sometimes there are
also supplements. When the bibliography is complex, you should always make use of both the table
of contents and any indexes. Remember too that
many bibliographies number their entries--always
verify whether the index indicates <u>page</u> number or
<u>item</u> number.

In general, the internal arrangement of these
bibliographies is also relatively uniform. For the
general bibliographies, there are sections on
"Généralités," followed by medieval literature,
sixteenth century literature, etc., each category
being subarranged alphabetically by author. Some of
the bibliographies listed below are continuing,
serial publications, usually appearing annually;
when this is the case, the title will be marked by
a star.

For other titles, look in your library's catalog under the following subject headings: "French literature--Bibliography," "French literature--Bibliography--First editions," "Bibliography--Early printed books," and "Festschriften--Bibliography--Indexes." You may also find suitable titles under "French fiction--Bibliography," "French poetry--Bibliography," and "French drama--Bibliography."

General

★ Cabeen, David Clark, ed. A Critical Bibliography of French Literature. Syracuse, New York: Syracuse University Press, 1947- .

Each volume in this series was compiled by a specialist in the field, and each is devoted to a particular period of literary activity. This multi-volume set not only lists books and periodicals articles, but also bibliographies of bibliographies, bibliographic guides, bibliographies, dissertations, and reviews. Since each volume was published at a different date, you will need to use the serially published general bibliographies listed below for comprehensiveness. The entries in this bibliography are annotated.

★ Klapp, Otto, ed. Bibliographie der französischen Literaturwissenschaft, 1956/58- . Frankfurt am Main: Klostermann, 1960- , v.1- .

---Supplement zu den Bänden I-VI (1956-1968). . . . Frankfurt am Main: Klostermann, 1970. Klapp is an important annual bibliography

which has indexes material in books, periodicals, Festschriften, and theses since 1956.
Both the table of contents and the chapter
headings are given in French and German. There
is an Index nominum (of scholars) and an Index
rerum (of subjects, including authors). The
index to volumes one through four was published separately in 1970.

★ Bibliographie de la littérature française du
    Moyen âge à nos jours. Edité par René Ran-
    cœur. Paris: A. Colin, 1966- .
    This serial bibliography continues Biblio-
graphie de la littérature française moderne
(sixteenth-twentieth centuries, 1962-65), and
Bibliographie littéraire (1953-61). Commonly
called "Rancœur," this annual compilation is
cumulated from the quarterly isses of the
journal Revue d'histoire littéraire de la
France. Because the items listed in the annual
are listed in this latter title each quarter,
Rancœur is the most up-to-date bibliography
available.

★ Modern Language Association of America. MLA
    International Bibliography of Books and
    Articles on the Modern Languages and Litera-
    tures. New York: The Association, 1921- .
    This standard bibliography includes a sec-
tion for French literature in its annual
volume. While adequate for the undergraduate,
both Klapp and Rancœur are more comprehensive
(and timely), and should be used when they are
available.

★ Romanische Bibliographie. Bibliographie

romane. <u>Romance Bibliography</u>. 1961/62- .
Tübingen: M. Niemeyer, 1967- .

This is a biennial bibliography for all of
the Romance languages and literatures which
lists scholarly publications for a two-year
period in either three or four volumes (with a
six- to seven-year lag in publication). Although the first two sets (1961-64) have subject headings in French, English, and German,
the third set is in German only. This title
continues the coverage of <u>Zeitschrift für</u>
<u>romanische Philologie. Supplement. Biblio-
graphie</u>.

★ <u>Year's Work in Modern Language Studies</u>.
Oxford: Modern Humanities Research Association, 1929/31- .

The section on French literature in this
annual publication is not comprehensive, but
like <u>Cabeen</u>, it is evaluative and critical.
The bibliography is in essay form and is useful
for indicating trends in literary criticism.
Unlike most of the bibliographies mentioned
thus far, the list of abbreviations and periodicals is at the back of the volume before the
index.

<u>Festschriften</u>

➤ Golden, Herbert Hershel, and Simches, Seymour
O. <u>Modern French Literature and Language:
A Bibliography of Homage Studies</u>. Cam-
bridge: Harvard University Press, 1953.

The <u>Festschrift</u>, a "homage" volume compiled
in honor of a scholar, is all too frequently
ignored by students when they search for re-

search materials, and yet it is an important
source of critical articles and essays. While
Festschriften are often now included in the
serial bibliographies, this index is useful as
a retrospective tool since it covers over 300
homage volumes.

Medieval

➤ Bédier, Joseph. Les Légendes épiques: Recherches sur la formation des chansons de
geste. . . . 3. éd. Paris: Champion,
1926-29.
This four-volume history of the chanson de
geste is not a bibliography, but does contain
extensive and useful bibliographical references
and is one of the standards of the field.

➤ Bossuat, Robert. Manuel bibliographique de la
littérature française du Moyen âge. Melun:
Librairie d'argences, 1951.
---Supplément, 1949-1953, avec le concours de
Jacques Monfrin, 1955.
---2e supplément, 1954-1960. 1961.
This is a specialized bibliographic guide
to medieval French literature which lists
editions, translations, and critical works in
two sections: l'ancien français and le moyen
français. Many of the entries in this work
are annotated and there is also a very useful
"Introduction à l'étude de la littérature
française du Moyen âge."

➤ Gautier, Léon. Bibliographie des chansons de
geste. (Complément des Epopées françaises.)
Paris: Welter, 1897.
This bibliography forms volume five of the

author's Les Epopées françaises and is divided
into two parts: a "bibliographie générale" and
a "bibliographie spéciale" which lists works
and criticism on individual chansons and
chansonniers. The entries are limited to works
published up to 1890.

➤ Jeanroy, Alfred. Bibliographie sommaire des
chansonniers français du Moyen âge (manu-
scrits et éditions). Paris: Champion,
1918.

The aim of this pamphlet-like work is to
supplement Raynaud's Bibliographie (see below).
The work is divided into two sections, the
first of which deals with manuscripts, the
second of which lists "éditions particulières."
An appendix lists "additions et rectifications
à la Liste des chansons de G. Raynaud."

➤ Raynaud, Gaston. Bibliographie des chansonniers français des XIIIe et XIVe siècles.
Paris: Vieweg, 1884.

This two-volume inventory of chansons will
be most useful to graduate students. Volume
one lists and describes manuscripts; volume
two lists individual chansons in alphabetical
order of rhymes, with references to manuscript.

➤ Woledge, Brian. Bibliographie des romans et
nouvelles en prose française antérieurs à
1500. Genève: Droz, 1954.

This bibliography of "romans et nouvelles"
alphabetically lists works, critical studies,
manuscripts, "éditions anciennes," "éditions
modernes," dates, and sources. There are also
supplementary tables of manuscripts, printers,

themes, etc.

Sixteenth Century

➤ Cioranescu, Alexandre. Bibliographie de la
littérature française du seizième siècle.
Paris: Klincksieck, 1959.
This is an important bibliography of materials about sixteenth century French literature. It is divided into two parts: "Généralités," which includes sections on "les
courants d'idées" and "le milieu historique,"
and "Auteurs," which lists works and critical
studies.

➤ Giraud, Jeanne. Manuel de bibliographie littéraire pour les XVIe XVIIe et XVIIIe siècles
français, 1921-1935. 2. éd. Paris: Vrin,
1958.
---1936-1945. Paris: Nizet, 1956.
---1946-1955. Paris: Nizet, 1970.
This work is divided into "Généralités" and
then into century, with subdivisions under
"Recueils de textes," "Etudes d'ensemble,"
"Questions particulières," and "Auteurs."
The two supplements are designed to supplement
not just the basic work, but also Lanson's
Manuel bibliographique (see below) and Thieme's
Bibliographie (see entry under "Nineteenth
Century").

➤ Lanson, Gustave. Manuel bibliographique de la
littérature française moderne, XVIe, XVIIe,
XVIIIe, et XIXe siècles. Nouv. éd. Paris:
Hachette, 1931.
This is an important bibliographic guide to
literary works, reference sources, and criti-

cal studies for French literature from 1500 to
1900. Glance at the detailed Table des
matières at the back of the volume and you will
have an idea of the richness of this selective
guide.

➤ Will, Samuel F. A Bibliography of American
   Studies on the French Renaissance (1500-
   1600). (Illinois Studies in Language and
   Literature, vol. 26, no. 2.) Urbana:
   University of Illinois Press, 1940.
   This is a short checklist of almost 1,900
books and periodical articles published in
the United States or written by Americans from
1886 to 1937 on all aspects of French history,
civilization, and literature.

Seventeenth Century

➤ Cioranescu, Alexandre. Bibliographie de la
   littérature française du dix-septième
   siècle. Paris: Centre national de la
   recherche scientifique, 1965-66.
   This three-volume bibliography is very
similar to the author's bibliography of sixteenth century French literature, although it
more heavily emphasizes literature. The index
to the bibliography is in volume three.

➤ Giraud, Jeanne. Manuel de bibliographie
   littéraire. . . . See entry in the category "Sixteenth Century."

➤ Lanson, Gustave. Manuel bibliographique. . . .
   See entry in the category "Sixteenth
   Century."

★ Modern Language Association of America.

92

French III. Bibliography of French Seventeenth Century Studies. Bloomington,
Indiana, [etc.], 1953-   .

This is an annual, noncumulative bibliography published by the MLA and known more
commonly as "French Three." The entries for
books and articles are annotated and reviews
are indicated.

Eighteenth Century

➤ Cioranescu, Alexandre. Bibliographie de la
littérature française du dix-huitième
siècle. . . . Paris: Centre national de
la recherche scientifique, 1969.

This three-volume set is similar in scope
to the author's bibliographies for the sixteenth and seventeenth centuries. The closing
date for entries in the bibliography is 1960.

➤ Escoffier, Maurice. Le Mouvement romantique,
1788-1850: Essai de bibliographie syn-
chronique et méthodique. Paris: Maison
du bibliophile, 1934.

Useful primarily to the graduate student,
Escoffier begins with a series of "Tables"
(noms d'auteurs, anonymes, recueils collectifs,
keepsakes et albums, périodiques, et relieurs)
followed by a "Catalogue du mouvement romantique" which covers from 1765 to 1882 in yearly
intervals, with subdivision by type of work:
poetry, fiction, literary history, religion,
etc.

➤ Giraud, Jeanne. Manuel de bibliographie
littéraire. . . . See entry in the category "Sixteenth Century."

➤ Lanson, Gustave. <u>Manuel bibliographique.</u> . . .
See entry in the category "Sixteenth
Century."

Nineteenth Century

➤ Escoffier, Maurice. <u>Le Mouvement romantique.</u> . . . See entry in the category
"Eighteenth Century."

➤ Lachèvre, Frédéric. <u>Bibliographie sommaire des
keepsakes et autres recueils collectifs de
la période romantique, 1823-1848.</u> (Les
Bibliographies nouvelles. Collection du
Bulletin du bibliophile.) Paris: Giraud-
Badin, 1929.
<u>Lachèvre</u>, like <u>Escoffier</u>, will be most use-
ful to the graduate student (or to the bibliophile) who is interested in "special editions."
The bibliography is in two volumes, with indexes at the back of each.

➤ Lanson, Gustave. <u>Manuel bibliographique.</u> . . .
See entry in the category "Sixteenth
Century."

➤ Modern Language Association of America. French
VI. Bibliography Committee. <u>French VI Bibliography: Critical and Biographical References for the Study of Nineteenth Century
French Literature.</u> New York: The Association, 1956-69.
This was a selective and noncumulative
serial bibliography which covered criticism
from 1954 through 1967. There is a table of
contents at the beginning of each issue, but
there is no index (which makes it somewhat

difficult to use).

 Talvart, Hector, and Place, Joseph. Bibliographie des auteurs modernes de langue
française (1800-1927). Paris: Editions
de la Chronique des lettres françaises,
1928- .

This is a very important bibliography of
nineteenth and twentieth century French
authors. Arranged alphabetically, it usually
gives a short biography, a list of the author's
works (including many minor publications), and
a list of critical works about the author.
Make sure to check the date of each volume,
since it contains listings only up to the time
of publication of that volume.

Thieme, Hugo Paul. Bibliographie de la
littérature française de 1800 à 1930. . . .
Paris: Droz, 1933.

Volumes one and two of this bibliography are
devoted to individual authors; volume three is
concerned with the history of French civilization. Thieme is continued by Dreher's
Bibliographie (see entry in the category
"Twentieth Century").

Twentieth Century

Dreher, Silpelitt, and Rolli, Madelin.
Bibliographie de la littérature française,
1930-1939. (Complément à la Bibliographie
de H. P. Thieme.) Genève: Droz, 1948-49.

This title continues the coverage of Thieme
(see entry in the category "Nineteenth Century") with the same scope. Dreher is continued by Drevet's Bibliographie (see page 96).

95

➤ Drevet, Marguerite L. Bibliographie de la littérature française, 1940-1949. (Complément à la Bibliographie de H. P. Thieme.) Genève: Droz, 1954-55.

Continues the scope and coverage of Dreher and Thieme (see above).

★ French XX Bibliography: Critical and Biographical References for French Literature since 1885. Vol. 5- , 1969- . New York: French Institute, 1969- .

French XX is a continuation of the MLA publication French VII (1949-1969) and appears annually. Coverage of critical materials begins in 1940, and this publication features the same type of arrangement and scope as French III (seventeenth century) and French VI (nineteenth century). Note that you will find references to some late nineteenth century authors (e.g., Zola, Maupassant, etc.), and that each entry is numbered consecutively, with many cross-references.

---Provençal Supplement. New York: French Institute, 1976.

This French XX supplement deals with Provençal literature from 1850 onwards, and indexes critical material from 1940 to the early 1970s.

➤ Talvart, Hector, and Place, Joseph. Bibliographie des auteurs modernes. . . . See entry in the category "Nineteenth Century."

➤ Thieme, Hugo Paul. Bibliographie de la littérature française. . . . See entry in the category "Nineteenth Century."

96

DISSERTATIONS

An important, and all too frequently overlooked information source for students of French literature is the doctoral dissertation. Although some of the bibliographies of literature and criticism do list relevant dissertations, it is difficult to ascertain just how comprehensive such listings may be, and so you need an understanding of the kinds of information sources that will give you access to dissertations.

Here in the United States, doctoral candidates at many colleges and universities send their dissertations to a central clearinghouse, University Microfilms, in Ann Arbor, Michigan. These dissertations, plus some Canadian and selected foreign dissertations, are abstracted in <u>Dissertation Abstracts International</u> (discussed in this section), and are available for purchase on microfilm or as "hard copy." If a dissertation is <u>not</u> available from University Microfilms, you may be able to obtain a copy through your library's interlibrary loan department. If you believe that you may have occasion to use any dissertations--and they are most likely to be useful for advanced research--you will need to allow several weeks for their arrival.

For other bibliographies and abstracts of dissertations, check in your library's catalog under the following subject headings: "Dissertations, Academic--France (or United States, Canada, Germany, etc.)," "Dissertations, Academic--Abstracts," and "France (or Germany, etc.)--Dissertations."

Bibliographies and Abstracts

United States

➤ American Doctoral Dissertations. Ann Arbor,
    Mich.: Xerox University Microfilms,
    1955/56- .

Formerly know as Index to American Doctoral
Dissertations, this bibliography is issued
annually as number thirteen of Dissertation
Abstracts International (see below), and lists
U.S. and Canadian dissertations not covered by
DAI such as those from Harvard University.

➤ Comprehensive Dissertation Index, 1861-1972.
    Ann Arbor, Mich.: Xerox University Micro-
    films, 1973.

The CDI in thirty-seven volumes lists most
American and some foreign dissertations for
the period 1861-1972. Volumes twenty-nine and
thirty are devoted to language and literature,
and the last four volumes are an author index
to the set.

➤ Dissertation Abstracts International. Ann
    Arbor, Mich.: Xerox University Microfilms,
    v.12- , 1952- .

Known until 1969 as Dissertation Abstracts,
this bibliography/abstracting service continues
the coverage of Microfilm Abstracts (volumes
one through ten, 1940-1951) with half-page
abstracts of those U.S. and Canadian dissertations submitted to University Microfilms.
Arranged alphabetically by broad subject field
(e.g., "Language and literature"), each entry
contains a full bibliographical description,
the abstract, and an order number for use if

wish to purchase a copy.

France

➤ France. Direction des bibliothèques de France.
Catalogue des thèses de doctorat soutenues
devant les universités françaises. Paris:
Cercle de la librairie, 1884/89-1958; nouvelle série, 1959- .
Until 1958, this official bibliography of
French dissertations was called the Catalogue
des thèses et écrits académiques. It is
arranged by université and subarranged by
faculté, and then by author's name. There are
author indexes since 1957.

➤ Bibliographie de la France: Supplément D.
Thèses. Paris, 1947- .
This supplement to the BF (see entry in the
section on "National and Trade Bibliographies")
is also arranged alphabetically by university.
and includes author and subject indexes.

BOOK REVIEWS

Book reviews can be very useful to you in
choosing the best scholarly editions of an author's
works or important critical studies. Happily, many
of the primary journals devoted to French literature regularly review new books.[4] Only a few of
them are cited here:

Australian Journal of French Studies. 1964- .
Diacritics. 1971- .
L'Esprit créateur. 1961- .
French Review. 1927- .
French Studies. 1947- .

99

Modern Language Notes. 1888-1961; MLN. 1962- .
Nouvelle revue française. 1909-43, 1953- .
Revue d'histoire littéraire de la France.
   1894- . (Remember that this journal also
   contains an important quarterly bibliography
   of literature and criticism!)
Revue des sciences humaines. 1927-31, 1933- .
Romance Philology. 1947- .
Romanic Review. 1910- .
Studi francesi. 1957- .

Besides these journals, there is also a monthly
periodical entitled Bulletin critique du livre
français (1945-) which lists and describes new
or recently published books in all fields of study.

Unfortunately, it is the happy few who can
regularly scan the journal literature for reviews
and other information (although you should try to
cultivate the habit), and so you may have occasion
to use the various book review indexes listed below.
For other review indexes, check in your library's
catalog under the heading "Books--Reviews" with the
following subdivisions: "--Indexes," "--Biblio-
graphy," and "--Periodicals." You may also find
important tools under the heading "Book selection
and bibliography--Best books."

Indexes

Bibliographie der Rezensionen, 1900-1943.
   Leipzig: Dietrich Verlag, 1901-44.
   This seventy-seven volume set lists book
reviews which appeared in almost 5,000 periodicals (3,000 in the German language, and the
remainder in other western European languages,
including English). While a knowledge of Ger-

man is not essential, it would be very helpful.

➤ Book Review Digest. New York: Wilson, 1906- .
   This is a monthly publication with annual
cumulations. While limited in scope to English
language periodicals, this information source
is very useful since it not only indexes book
reviews, but also gives some excerpts from many
of the reviews--a timesaving feature if the
book you are interested in has been reviewed
in several periodicals.

➤ Book Review Index. Detroit: Gale Research,
   v.1-   , 1965- .
   This monthly index (with quarterly and
annual cumulations) is, like Book Review
Digest, limited to English language periodicals, but is a standard title to be found in
almost every reference department.

➤ Index to Book Reviews in the Humanities.
   Detroit: Thomson, v.1-   , 1960- .
   This annual index includes some foreign
language periodicals within its purview, and
is limited to more "scholarly" reviews than
either Book Review Digest or Book Review
Index.

➤ Internationale Bibliographie der Rezensionen
   wissenschaftlicher Literatur. Osnabrück:
   Dietrich Verlag, 1971- .
   International in scope and coverage, this
index is important for its coverage of western
European book reviews of scholarly literature.
Instructions and prefatory matter are in Ger-
man, English, and French.

101

GUIDES TO SPECIAL COLLECTIONS

Whether you are an undergraduate keenly interested in pursuing an advanced degree in French
drama, or a graduate student concerned with library
resources and archival collections in Europe, you
will want to be aware of the various guides to
special collections which are available in most
reference departments. These guides also serve to
remind you that you are not limited to the resources
of your own campus library.

For other guides, check in your library's
catalog under the heading "Library resources--
Directories."

➤ Ash, Lee. Subject Collections: A Guide to
Special Book Collections and Subject Em-
phases as Reported by University, College,
Public, and Special Libraries in the United
States and Canada. 4th ed. New York:
Bowker, 1974.

Arranged by subject headings (e.g., "French
poetry"), this work contains approximately
35,000 references to special book collections.

➤ Downs, Robert Bingham. American Library Re-
sources: A Bibliographical Guide. Chicago:
American Library Association, 1951.
---Supplement, 1950-1961. 1962.
---Supplement, 1961-1970. 1972.

Downs lists published bibliographies of
special materials with entries arranged by
the Dewey Decimal Classification system (see
Figure 6 on pages 20 and 21). There is an index for author, subject, and library.

➤ Lewanski, Richard Casimir. Subject Collections

in European Libraries: A Directory and
Bibliographical Guide.   New York: Bowker,
1965.

Like Downs, Lewanski is arranged by Dewey
Decimal and then subarranged alphabetically
by country.   The index is in English, French,
and German.

NOTES

1. For further information on this remarkable dictionary, see the two reviews which appeared in the
Times Literary Supplement (TLS) on August 3, 1973,
p. 909, and October 13, 1972, p. 1229.

2. The Laffont-Bompiani titles mentioned in this
section are based upon the Italian Dizionario
letterario Bompiani delle opere e dei personnagi di
tutti i tempi e di tutte le letterature (Milan:
Bompiani, 1947-50, nine volumes) and Dizionario
universale della letteratura contemporanea (Milan:
Mondadori, 1959-63, five volumes).   If you have
reading competence in Italian, you will find these
titles to be more comprehensive than the French
abridgments.

3. Many of the largest research libraries have also
published their catalogs.   Also, as libraries con-
tinue to participate in automation projects, many
new kinds of bibliographic tools are becoming
available.   An excellent example of this is the
Harvard University Widener Shelflist series.   Numbers forty-seven and forty-eight of this series,
French Literature, were published in 1973.

4. For more information about journals devoted to
French literature, see Louise A. Fiber's "A

Selected Guide to Journals in the Field of French
Language and Literature" which appeared in <u>French
Review</u> (Vol. 47, pp. 1128-1141) in May of 1974.
She lists and describes ninety-one United States
and Canadian journals.

3 USING YOUR TIME EFFECTIVELY: THE MECHANICS OF RESEARCH

At this point you know something about the library and the primary reference tools devoted to French literature. This final chapter is devoted to a discussion of how this knowledge can be put to work to help you use your limited time in a profitable way when it is time to begin work on a term paper. But before we begin our examination of some of the practical aspects of library researching, you should also be aware of the existence of those works which will help you to understand just what the term paper and literary research are all about. The following titles may serve as a useful introduction. Turn to your professors for other recommendations.

➤ Altick, Richard D. The Art of Literary Research. Revised ed. New York: Norton, 1975.

While written for the student of English and American literature, this work has much to say to any student of belles lettres about the meaning of scholarship.

➤ Altick, Richard D. The Scholar Adventurers. New York: Free Press, 1966, c1950.

A fascinating and absorbing account of
literary detective work. You cannot but feel
happy about having chosen literature as a
field of study when you read this book.

➤ Bénac, Henri. Guide pour la recherche des
    idées dans les dissertations et les études
    littéraires. Paris: Hachette, 1961.

This work serves both as a standard introduction to the French methodology of scholarship and as a practical glossary of literary
terminology. To quote Bénac: "Notre Guide
vise à aider l'élève au moment précis de son
travail où, après avoir compris le sens exact
du sujet et ramené celui-ci à un certain nom-
bre de questions qui lui serviront de plan de
recherche, il tente de découvrir des idées qui
leur fourniront une réponse."

➤ Chassang, A., and Senninger, Ch. La Disser-
    tation littéraire générale: Classes
    supérieures de Lettres et Enseignement
    Supérieur. Paris: Hachette, 1955.

While somewhat dated, this guide gives many
examples of possible term paper topics and exam
questions, and leads the student step by step
in a detailed analysis of those questions.
After the general introduction, the book is
divided into three parts: "De l'œuvre littéraire: le lecteur, l'auteur," "Des écoles aux
tendances," and "Les grands genres littéraires."

➤ Thorpe, James, ed. The Aims and Methods of
    Scholarship in Modern Languages and Litera-
    tures. 2nd ed. New York: Modern Lan-
    guage Association of America, c1970.

This eighty-one page pamphlet contains four important essays by eminent critics on linguistics, textual criticism, literary history, and literary criticism.

GETTING READY FOR RESEARCH

The term has not yet begun, but this is precisely the time to get some of the preliminaries out of the way before things get too hectic. Among the various activities which will help you to "get ready for research" are:

1. Buying the supplies you will need during the term. This will probably include:
   A. an ample quantity of index cards (more about this later);
   B. pencils, pens, notebook and typewriter paper;
   C. a fresh, new typewriter ribbon.

2. Choosing a style manual and reading it through so as to familiarize yourself with the many complicated rules for bibliographic citation. Usually, your professors will be very happy if you use the Modern Language Association's MLA Style Sheet (2nd ed.; New York: MLA, 1970). If you are doing advanced research for a masters or doctoral degree, you may also want to consult the more detailed A Manual of Style (12th ed., revised; Chicago: University of Chicago Press, 1969, and commonly referred to as the "Chicago Manual of Style").

3. Taking a tour of your library. Make sure you know in advance where the reference desk

and card catalog are. Wander through the reference area and note where the dictionaries, encyclopedias, and standard bibliographic tools are shelved. Browse through the stacks in the area where works of and about French literature are shelved. All of this sound simplistic, but too few students take the short amount of time necessary to familiarize themselves with their library's physical layout. It will save you time later, so do it now.

4. Stake out a quiet place where you can study, read, and take notes, both in the library and at home.

5. Make sure that you have an adequate "home reference library" which should include an authoritative French dictionary, a French-English dictionary, a sound, one-volume history of French literature, and perhaps a good book on usage and/or a grammar. Remember, your library is not likely to be open twenty-four hours a day, so such a "core" library for your personal use will probably pay for itself many times over. If you are "momentarily lacking funds" (and who isn't these days), find out if your library either circulates older editions of standard reference tools or "rents" books at a nominal fee; you might be pleasantly surprised!

THE TERM BEGINS

It is the first day of the new term, and you

have enrolled in a course on André Gide. Your professor has handed out the reading list and discussed the fifteen to twenty page term paper he expects to have in the last week of the term. Before beginning his introductory lecture on Gide, your professor mentions that he wants to see each student individually sometime during the first two weeks of classes in order to discuss his or her choice of term paper topic.

Before panic sets in, it is time to reflect on the two cardinal rules of effective library researching: (1) Start early, and (2) Be systematic. If you follow both of these rules assiduously, you should have little difficulty in keeping up with all of the various demands on your time. Do not assume, as do so many students, that most--perhaps even all--of your work must come during the last weeks of the semester or quarter. It should not! Everyone starts off with the best of intentions, and promises that "This time, I'm going to start early!", but relatively few actually keep their promise. Scholarship demands discipline and hard work, and can be enjoyed and appreciated to its fullest only if you allow yourself enough time to do so. And if this isn't reason enough for you to start early, remember that you may need some materials which are not available in your library: interlibrary loan, as we noted in Chapter 1, is a process which can easily consume several weeks.

Now that you've decided to start early, it's time to be systematic. What exactly do you have to do in the coming weeks before you actually sit down and write that paper for your class on Gide? You will first have to choose your topic, then compile

a bibliography, and finally read and take notes.
The remainder of this chapter will be devoted to an
examination of the first two activities.

CHOOSING A TOPIC

Your professor has just closed his manila
folder, and the first lecture on Gide is over. Time
for coffee? Perhaps, but only if you grab a cup on
your way to the library where your most difficult
task awaits you: choosing a topic for your paper.
Let us assume for the sake of illustration that you
have never before heard of André Gide (unlikely, but
possible!). Where will you begin in the seemingly
hopeless task of choosing a topic in this, the first
week of the term? Begin with your class notes:
did the overview of <u>L'Immoraliste</u> intrigue you? how
about Gide's relationship with his contemporaries?
Doubtless, several points covered in the first
lecture interest you. Now you must do some reading
about Gide to further refine that interest.

You go directly to the card catalog, and, under
the subject heading "Gide, André Paul Guillaume,
1869-1951," you find over thirty books listed.
Which should you pick for an introduction to his
life and work? After having read about the catalog
in Chapter 1, it should be clear that most of the
information on the catalog card will help you to
narrow your choice of likely titles. You can probably eliminate immediately the extremely long or
multi-volume works; remember, you're interested in
a <u>brief</u> overview to complement the class lecture.
You will probably want a recently published work of
some 200 pages, by a respected author, that has a
good bibliography, and that was published by a

110

reputable firm (e.g., the university presses).
After reading through the entries in the catalog,
you finally decide to examine four titles: Germaine Brée's Gide, Albert J. Guérard's André Gide,
Vinio Rossi's André Gide, and Thomas Cordle's André
Gide.

You will certainly not have enough time to read
all four of these books, but the catalog can only
tell you so much about them. The final choice of
one book over another will have to be based upon a
personal examination of each of the titles. Examine
each book by scanning the table of contents, the
index, and the bibliography. Note whether or not
there are any special features associated with one
or more of the titles (three of them have a chronology of Gide's life). Skim through the preface or
introduction to the book. Who seems to be the
intended audience? Is it readable?

After some fifteen to twenty minutes of evaluation, you're ready to make a choice. Personally,
I would select Cordle's André Gide (New York:
Twayne Publishers, 1969) for the following reasons:
it is of "average" length (185 pages) and will only
take a few hours to read; its purpose is made clear
in a short introduction to the series of which it
is a part (the Twayne World Authors Series): "The
intent of each volume in these series is to present
a critical-analytical study of the works of the
writer; . . ."; it has a chronology of Gide's life
and a good index; and it includes a detailed bibliography of primary sources (works by Gide), subdivided by type of work, and secondary sources
(works about Gide), also subdivided into such
categories as "general works," "more limited

111

studies," "bibliographical studies," etc. This is
probably exactly what you need to get started in
choosing a topic.

While reading through your introduction to
Gide and his work, you have probably been literally
assailed by possible ideas for a paper, many of
which you have hastily jotted down. Are you still
interested in studying, say, L'Immoraliste? If so,
what aspects particularly interest you: character
development? narrative technique? plot structure?
the influence of Nietzche on Gide's ideas as ex-
pressed in the novel? Obviously, there are in-
numerable possibilities for an interesting and in-
formative paper. Your choice of one over another
will be dependent on several factors:

1. Is your initial choice of topic too broad
   or narrow to handle given the limitations
   of a fifteen to twenty page paper?
2. Will you find most of the materials you
   will need in your campus library or nearby
   at another college?
3. What interests you the most? Since you will
   be living with your choice for ten to
   twenty weeks, you want to have chosen a
   topic which will stimulate you.

For answers to the first two questions, you
may want to consult your professor. Tell him what
you have read thus far, and where your general
interests lie. He will be able to tell you whether
or not the library's resources are adequate. As
you ponder the last question, keep this in mind:
your professor is probably not as concerned with
what the topic is as much as he is interested in

112

how you handle it. Unless otherwise instructed, you can safely assume that your professor does not want to see a twenty-page editorial of personal opinion or a "scissors and paste job" which reports what other critics have to say about your topic. Most likely, he expects you to conduct a literary investigation into a topic and illustrate thereby that you have gained a command of your subject and of the various resources you used to thoroughly research it. Your topic will, of course, be re- fined and clarified during the research process, but this initial choice is in itself half the battle.

COLLECTING YOUR SOURCES

You have read L'Immoraliste and one short monograph on Gide, and you have chosen a topic for your paper, all this within two or three days of the beginning of the term. Now it's back to the library where many hours (spread over several days) of bibliographic searching must begin. Before you consider what you will be searching for, give some thought to how you will record what you find. Most experienced library researchers would probably recommend using index cards.

There are probably as many systems for using index cards to compile a bibliography and to take notes as there are individual researchers. The kind of system you develop for yourself will need to be based on your own personal habits and temperament, and the demands posed by the kind of investigation you are undertaking. A system which you may find to be quite practical is to use 5 x 8 inch index cards. On the recto of the card (the unruled side), copy down the complete citation in the bibliographic format specified by one of the standard style manuals. By copying down the full citation now, you will later be able to alphabetize your cards and easily type up the bibliography for your paper, thus saving time. Leave space to the left for your library's call number, and some space at the bottom where you can write the source from which you gleaned the citation (e.g., "MLA 1970"). On the verso of the card (the ruled side), you will take notes.

You will find on your shopping trip to the stationery department that index cards come in a variety of colors. Differently colored cards can be used for many purposes. You can pick one color over another for the form of the reference you are using (e.g., primary vs. secondary, journal article vs. book), or by its anticipated use in your paper. Using colored cards to distinguish the form of the reference is very useful when combined with colored tabs for subdivision by anticipated use. For example, each card might be marked with a red metal or plastic tab if the reference deals with Gide's own feelings about the characters in his novel, and with green tabs if character interaction if the subject, or by both if both ideas are discussed.

An alternative to the one-card system is one in which smaller 3 x 5 inch index cards are used for the bibliographic citation, call number, etc., with notes being transcribed on notebook-sized paper. With this system, though, you will need some kind of cross-referencing index since your citation is located in one place and your notes in another. At the top of each card you would write--

in pencil, should you decide to change it later--a
brief précis of the subject such as "G's relationship with Martin du Gard--Influence."

Regardless of the "system" you choose for
gathering citations and notes, don't go to campus
without some cards and/or your notebook: copying
down important information willy-nilly on whatever
happens to be handy can be disastrous later when you
can't remember where you wrote it. Also, give some
thought to how you can physically protect your cards
and papers. If you use a card system, you can buy
vinyl-covered carrying cases for cards of any size;
such portable carriers are less bulky than index
card boxes, they insure that all the information
you need is readily available, and that your important notes won't be scattered or destroyed by your
carelessness, freakish weather, or acts of God.

Having chosen a bibliographic and note-taking
system, it is now time to begin your search for
sources. Here, the second axiom of effective
library researching becomes particularly important:
be systematic in your approach. Consider what you
are looking for and where you will find it. First
of all, you will be looking for primary sources:
you will want to identify those works by Gide which
will serve as necessary background for your paper,
such as personal notes and correspondence. Among
the primary sources you seek, also include an
authoritative, critical edition of L'Immoraliste.
Usually, professors will have asked you to buy in-
expensive, paperbound editions of the titles included
on your reading list. These are perfectly suitable
for portable reading copies, but cannot be used as
a reliable primary source for use in your paper

since they are rarely as well edited and annotated as the standard scholarly editions. With experience, you will come to learn that editions such as those published by Gallimard in the "Bibliothèque de la Pléiade" series are reliable.

After you have found and listed the primary sources, you will need to compile a list of <u>second-ary sources</u>: those works about Gide and your topic. Remember that these secondary sources will be scattered in journals, <u>Festschriften</u>, books, and dissertations. Depending on your own background and knowledge of twentieth century literature, you may also want to include in your search for second-ary sources a general history of the period to help you place Gide's work in a historical context.

Knowing now what materials you need, the question of where you will obtain access to these materials arises. After having read Chapter 2, you probably have a good idea of where to logically begin: with the bibliographic guides and the bib-liographies of bibliographies. From these tools you will get the titles of separately published bibliographies and information on reliable primary sources.

In order to insure that your information is up-to-date, you will also want to consult the serially published bibliographies. Decide now which bibliographies you will need to consult (e.g., <u>Rancœur</u>, <u>MLA</u>, <u>Klapp</u>), and jot down all the titles on a separate index card or sheet of paper in the order in which you plan to use them. As you com-plete your searching of each title, make sure that you check off that title on your "master list." By the same token, if you should be interrupted in your searching, remember to jot down next to a title the years <u>already</u> searched.

How far must you search through the bibliographies? The answer to this depends mainly on how extensive your project is and how much time you have to devote to it. Obviously, for a term paper, you are not expected to compile an exhaustive bibliography worthy of appendage to a dissertation or thesis. Within the limits you set for yourself, however, you must be thorough. Since Gide's works are continually being published in new editions, your search for primary sources will necessarily be more detailed and comprehensive than your search for secondary sources, which can be limited to a specific period of time, say, for example, from 1940 or 1950 to the present.

A more practical consideration in how far you will search through various bibliographies is whether or not there are separately published bibliographies on your subject. If, for example, a relatively comprehensive bibliography of primary and/ or secondary sources on Gide was published in 1967, you will only have to search through the serially published bibliographies back to that date. But pay careful attention to the "comprehensiveness" of such a bibliography: read through the preface carefully to discover just how systematically the tool was compiled. The best bibliographies will have explanations as to how they were compiled, and from what sources. If such prefatory and explanatory material is lacking, be wary of depending on it for accurate information.

How many citations should you cull from the bibliographies you decide to use? Again, the answer

depends on the scope of your project and the time
allotted to it.   But remember, if you are to err,
err on the side of copying down too many citations.
Unless you happen to studying at a Harvard, Yale,
or Berkeley, your library will probably not have
all of the titles you need, and so if you copy down
more than you anticipate using now, you will save
time later when you don't have to return to the
drudgery of searching through bibliographies.

   If you have budgeted your time well, you should
have finished compiling a list of sources within a
week to a week and a half of the first lecture.
Now is the time for you to arrange your cards in
alphabetical order and search for your sources in
the catalog.   Copy down the complete call number on
the recto of each card.   When you have finished your
search in the catalog, sit down and look through
your cards for titles you did not find.   Separate
them out and decide which ones seem to be essential
to your topic; for these, you will have to submit
interlibrary loan requests.

   The remainder of the term will be spent in
reading, taking notes, and thinking about your
topic, with approximately one week given to the
actual organizing and writing of the paper.   If you
proceed systematically and allow certain hours each
week to be given over to work on your paper, and if
you use the various reference tools discussed in
Chapter 2 wisely, by the time the end of the term
is near, your paper should practically write itself.

A CONCLUDING NOTE

   During the course of an average term, you will
have occasion to use a variety of reference tools

such as dictionaries, encyclopedias, glossaries of
literary terminology, and grammars. This Introduction to Library Research in French Literature is
only the beginning of what should become your own
continuing education program in the use of these
tools. As your knowledge of literature increases,
so too should your knowledge of reference sources.
The best scholars continually seek to develop and
enrich their awareness of the bibliographic apparatus of the field--it saves them time and increases
their chances of producing sound scholarship. Further, you should find yourself in a position to
discuss the merits and faults not just of literature, but also of those tools which are designed to
serve you in your scholarly endeavors. As you come
across a new reference tool that seems likely to be
useful at some future time, make a note of it on an
index card with a brief description of its positive
and negative features. You will certainly be saving
the cards used for research on term papers and
other projects to compile a personal bibliography
for future use; why not also compile a personal
bibliography of useful reference tools?

As you work on various papers, remember too
that you will inevitably need to consult certain
reference tools outside the realm of those devoted
purely to French literature. You may have occasion
to write a paper on the influence of a German
novelist on a French poet, or to study broader
questions such as the influence of cinema on literature. The student of literature often has occasion
to wander into other fields such as psychology,
philosophy, and religion. There are thousands of
reference works available which can help you to

gain access to information on such subjects, and your preliminary thoughts on what materials you need, which tools to use, and how far to go in searching will necessarily be affected.

Learning to use the library and its resources effectively is learning how to better use your own time. The measure of how well you succeed in mastering these resources will be reflected in the grades on your papers, and in your own satisfaction with an ever-increasing degree of thoroughness. Bonne chance!

AUTHOR-TITLE INDEX

This author-title index, unlike the card catalog, is arranged alphabetically in the "letter by
letter" mode. Thus, you will find "Bonnard, Jean"
before "Bon usage, Le" (the opposite would be found
in your library's catalog). Numbers are filed
as though they were spelled out, and so you would
find "French III" after "French VI." Abbreviations
(e.g., MLA or MLN) are filed as if they were words.

For access to the subject content of this
work, see the Contents.

§   §   §

Abraham, Pierre, 69
Académie des inscriptions et belles-lettres, 68
Académie française, Paris, 39
Adam, Antoine, 67
Aims and Methods of Scholarship in the Modern Lan-
    guages and Literatures, The, 106-107
Albérès, R. M., 65
Altfranzösisches Wörterbuch. See Tobler-Lommatzsch,
    Altfranzösisches Wörterbuch
Altick, Richard D., 105
American Doctoral Dissertations, 98
American Library Resources: A Bibliographical

122

123

1823-1848, 94

Bibliography of American Studies on the French
  Renaissance (1500-1600), A, 92

"Bibliography of French Literary History: Progress,
  Problems, Projects, The," 72

Bibliography of French Seventeenth Century Studies,
  93

Bibliothèque nationale. See Paris. Bibliothèque
  nationale

Biographie universelle, 64

Bloch, Oscar, 48

Bock, Gerhard, 75

Boisdeffre, Pierre de, 65

Bompiani, Valentino, 62

Bonnard, Jean, 43

Bon usage, Le, 58-59

Book Review Digest, 101

Book Review Index, 101

Books in Print, 83

Bossuat, Robert, 89

Bouvier, Emile, 71

Braun, Sidney David, 61

Brereton, Geoffrey, 67

Britannica. See Encyclopedia Britannica

British Museum. Department of Printed Books, 79

Brown, J. Buchanan-. See Buchanan-Brown, J.

Brunet, Gustave, 84

Brunet, Jacques Charles, 80

Buchanan-Brown, J., 61

Bulletin critique du livre français, 100

Cabeen, David Clark, 86

Calvet, Jean, 68

Carrère, Marcel, 52

Cassell's Encyclopedia of World Literature, 61

126

Larousse Modern French-English (English-French)
   Dictionary, 55

Larousse, Pierre, 42

Lasserre, Emilie, 59

Légendes épiques: Recherches sur la formation des
   chansons de geste, Les, 89

Leitner, Moses Jonathon, 51

Lerminier, Georges, 67

Leroud, Alain, 45

Lewanski, Richard Casimir, 102

Lexique de la langue de Molière comparée à celle des
   des écrivains de son temps, 46-47

Lexique de la langue du dix-septième siècle. See
   Français classique: Lexique de la langue du
   dix-septième siècle, Le

Lexique de l'ancien français, 43

Library of Congress. See United States. Library of
   Congress

Literary Terms: A Dictionary, 56

Littérature française (Adam, et al.), 67

Littérature française (Bédier-Hazard), 67, 69

Littérature française: Collection, 69

Littérature française contemporaine, 1827-1849, La,
   82

Littératures françaises, connexes et marginales, 70

Littré, Emile, 40-41

Livet, Charles Louis, 46

Livres de l'année--Biblio, Les, 83

Livres de la semaine, Les, 83

Livres du mois, Les, 83

Livres du semestre, Les, 83

Livres du trimestre, Les, 83

Lommatzsch, Erhard, 44

McCoy, F. N., xv

Monfrin, Jacques, 89
Morot-Sir, Edouard, 67
Mots et les associations d'idées, Les. See
    Dictionnaire alphabétique et analogique de la
    langue française
Mouvement romantique, 1788-1850: Essai de biblio-
    graphie synchronique et méthodique, Le, 93
National Union Catalog, 36
National Union Catalog: A Cumulative Author List,
    78-79
National Union Catalog: Pre-1956 Imprints, 78
New Cassell's French Dictionary: French-English,
    English-French, 55
New French-English Dictionary of Slang and Collo-
    quialisms, The, 51-52
New Serial Titles, 36
Nouveau dictionnaire des difficultés du français,
    57-58
Nouveau dictionnaire étymologique et historique,
    48-49
Nouveau dictionnaire national des contemporains, 64
Nouveau petit Larousse, 42
Nouvelle revue française, 100
Osburn, Charles B., 73, 74
Oxford Companion to French Literature, The, 63. See
    also Concise Oxford Dictionary of French
    Literature, The
Paris. Bibliothèque nationale, 77
Petit de Julleville, Louis, 69
Petit dictionnaire de l'ancien français, 44
Petit glossaire des classiques français du dix-
    septième siècle, 46
Petit Larousse. See Nouveau petit Larousse
Petit Robert. See Dictionnaire alphabétique et

analogique de la langue française (abridged)

Pichois, Claude, 69

Pingaud, Bernard, 63

Place, Joseph, 95

Précis de grammaire française, 59

Present State of French Studies: A Collection of
    Research Reviews, The, 74

Queneau, Raymond, 70

Quérard, Joseph Marie, 82, 84

Rancœur, René, 87

Raynaud, Gaston, 90

Redfern, James, 60

Reid, Joyce M. H., 61

Répertoire bibliographique des livres imprimés en
    France au seizième siècle, 81

Research and Reference Guide to French Studies, 73

Researching and Writing in History, xv

Revue des sciences humaines, 100

Revue d'histoire littéraire de la France, 87, 100

Rheims, Maurice, 47

Robert, Paul, 41, 42

Rolli, Madelin, 95

Romance Bibliography, 87-88

Romance Philology, 100

Romanic Review, 100

Romanische Bibliographie, 87-88

Salmon, Amédée, 43

Sandry, Géo, 52

Scholar Adventurers, The, 105-106

"Selected Guide to Journals in the Field of French
    Language and Literature, A," 103-104

Senninger, Ch., 106

Shaw, Harry, 56

Sheehy, Eugene P., 70